ADVERTISING'S WAR ON TERRORISM

D1004066

The Story of the U.S. State Department's Shared Values Initiative

OTHER BOOKS OF INTEREST FROM MARQUETTE BOOKS

Mitchell Land and Bill W. Hornaday, *Contemporary Media Ethics: A Practical Guide for Students, Scholars and Professionals* (2006). ISBN: 0-922993-41-6 (cloth); 0-922993-42-4 (paperback)

Stephen D. Cooper, *Watching the Watchdog: Bloggers as the Fifth Estate* (2006). ISBN: 0-922993-46-7 (cloth); 0-922993-47-5 (paperback)

Joey Reagan, *Applied Research Methods for Mass Communicators* (2006). ISBN: 0-922993-45-9

Ralph D. Berenger (ed.), *Cybermedia Go to War: Role of Alternative Media During the 2003 Iraq War* (2006). ISBN: 0-922993-24-6

David Demers, *Dictionary of Mass Communication: A Guide for Students, Scholars and Professionals* (2005). ISBN: 0-922993-35-1 (cloth); 0-922993-25-4 (paperback)

John Burke, *From Prairie to Palace: The Lost Biography of Buffalo Bill* (2005). Introduction by Dr. Jason Berger; edited by Tim Connor. ISBN: 0-922993-21-1

John C. Merrill, Ralph D. Berenger and Charles J. Merrill, *Media Musings: Interviews with Great Thinkers* (2004). ISBN: 0-922993-15-7

Ralph D. Berenger (ed.), *Global Media Go to War: Role of Entertainment and News During the 2003 Iraq War* (2004). ISBN: 0-922993-10-6

Melvin L. DeFleur and Margaret H. DeFleur, *Learning to Hate Americans: How U.S. Media Shape Negative Attitudes Among Teenagers in Twelve Countries* (2003). ISBN: 0-922993-05-X

David Demers (ed.), *Terrorism, Globalization and Mass Communication: Papers Presented at the 2002 Center for Global Media Studies Conference* (2003). ISBN: 0-922993-04-1

ADVERTISING'S

WAR on TERRORISM

The Story of the U.S. State Department's Shared Values Initiative

JAMI A. FULLERTON
ALICE G. KENDRICK

MARQUETTE BOOKS
Spokane, Washington

Library of Congress Cataloging-in-Publication Data

Fullerton, Jami A., 1963-
    Advertising's war on terrorism : the story of the U.S. State Department's
Shared Values Initiative / Jami A. Fullerton, Alice G. Kendrick.
       p. cm.
    Includes bibliographical references and index.
    ISBN-13: 978-0-922993-43-7 (hardcover : alk. paper)
    ISBN-10: 0-922993-43-2 (hardcover : alk. paper)
    ISBN-13: 978-0-922993-44-4 (pbk : alk. paper)
    ISBN-10: 0-922993-44-0 (pbk. : alk. paper)
       1.United States--Relations--Arab countries. 2. Arab countries--Relations--
United States. 3. Shared Values Initiative. 4. War on Terrorism, 2001-- Public
opinion. 5. United States--Foreign public opinion, Arab. 6. Public relations
and politics--United States. 7. Public relations and politics--Arab countries. I.
Kendrick, Alice. II. Title.
    DS63.2.U5F85 2006
    327.1'40973--dc22

                                                    2006003231

Marquette Books
3107 East 62nd Avenue
Spokane, Washington 99223
509-443-7057 (voice) / 509-448-2191 (fax)
books@marquettebooks.org / www.MarquetteBooks.org

Table of Contents

Foreword, 7

Dedication and Acknowledgments, 9

Introduction, 11

Chapters

    1. A Brief History of the Shared Values Initiative, 19

    2. The Shared Values Initiative: Propaganda or Public Diplomacy? 43

    3. New Approaches to Public Diplomacy, 75

    4. Reactions to the Shared Values Initiative, 101

    5. Did Shared Values Work? The Post-Campaign Study, 137

    6. Did Shared Values Work? Results of Experiments and Diagnostic Copy Tests, 167

    7. Advertising: A Weapon for the War on Terrorism? 195

Appendix A — SVI Storyboards, 217

Appendix B — "Don't Brand the U.S., Uncle Sam: The Backlash Against Charlotte Beers' America Branding," by John Brown, 229

Appendix C — "Public Diplomacy: What Have We Learned?" by Joe B. Johnson, 235

Selected Bibliography, 241

Index, 249

Foreword

Many book manuscripts have passed over my desk in the last four years, but none can match this one in terms of the concerns it raises about competence in our government and news media. The evidence presented by professors Jami Fullerton and Alice Kendrick suggests that Bush Administration officials missed an opportunity to improve America's image in the Arab and Muslim worlds because they acted upon ideological and parochial prejudices rather than upon scientific evidence. More specifically, the evidence shows that:

- Many U.S. Department of State bureaucrats, politicians, journalists and academics denounced the Shared Values Initiative public diplomacy campaign even though they had no good scientific evidence to back up their criticism.
- Some State Department bureaucrats undermined SVI through off-the-record and background interviews with journalists, whose stories often failed to accurately portray the goals of the campaign.
- Some State Department bureaucrats belittled the creator of SVI—Under Secretary Charlotte Beers, a former advertising executive—simply because she was an "outsider" who had new and different ideas.
- State Department bureaucrats, including Beers, created a nonprofit organization apparently for the purpose of concealing the identity of the real sponsor of the SVI television commercials, which was the State Department. Some media scholars say this act is unethical.
- Many State Department bureaucrats have little knowledge about mass communication research and theories, even though they

supposedly are in the business of promoting America's image to the world.

- Some State Department bureaucrats refused requests from the authors of this book for basic public information about the Shared Values Initiative. They cited the Smith-Mundt Act to defend their actions, but they have provided no good evidence to justify this position. The decision to deny access appears to be motivated by a desire to suppress information that could embarrass State Department officials.

The cynicism these actions generate in me is tempered only by the knowledge that not everyone in government or in journalism is incompetent in all things all of the time. In hindsight, former Secretary of State Colin L. Powell appears to have used extremely good judgment in hiring Beers and launching the "Brand America" campaign. He recognized the importance of using communication science in public diplomacy. The only big mistake he made was assuming that State Department bureaucrats and U.S. ambassadors also would recognize an opportunity when they saw it.

Former U.S. Ambassador to Syria Christopher Ross and former diplomat Joe B. Johnson also demonstrated sound judgment. Their even-handed critiques of SVI, which are discussed in Chapter 4 of this book, show that each has the ability to sift wheat from chaff—a skill that presumably is a prerequisite for a competent diplomat.

Many lessons are to be learned from SVI, and Professors Fullerton and Kendrick do an outstanding job of presenting them in this book, especially in the last chapter. I only emphasize here that dogma is the greatest enemy of not only science, but of government and journalism as well. As philosopher Immanuel Kant put it: "The death of dogma is the birth of reality."

—Dr. David Demers, publisher and associate professor of mass communication, Edward R. Murrow School of Communication, Washington State University

Dedication and Acknowledgments

I dedicate this book to Dr. Maureen Nemecek, who was the first to show me the wonders of the Muslim world, and to my students there, who helped me realize that while not everyone lives and thinks like an American, we share values that bring us together in important and powerful ways.

I also extend special thanks to my in-laws and siblings, who showed their support by babysitting so I could write; to my precious Helen, who hopefully won't have to go to the babysitter so often now that I'm finished; and to my husband Sam, whose loving actions speak very loudly.—JF

I dedicate this work to Aunt Ellie, who every Sunday afternoon decades ago would take time to share her news magazines and her views on world events.

I thank Jay and Sara for their interest in and tolerance of mom's big writing project and Kevin for his support and patience.—AK

Our mutual gratitude goes to a number of friends and colleagues who helped make this book possible. They include Bruce Bendinger, Sheri Broyles, Cari Eggspuehler and Peter Noble.

Thanks also to Maridel Allinder, Patty Alvey, Greg Bartlett, Andrea Choquette, Renat Deushev, Shakhboz Eshpulatov, Matthew

Hamilton, Kevin Keenan, Nicole Nascenzi, Richard Nelson, Judy Noble, Hal Williams, Tom Reichert, Steve Rhom, Amanda Taylor, Tom Weir, OSU College of Arts & Sciences Summer Research Grant Program, OSU-Tulsa Center for Instruction Technology (Larry Cochran, Earl Gorden and Brian Nuttall), OSU-Tulsa Librarian Lynn Wallace, SMU Office of Research and Graduate Studies, Richter Foundation and SMU Meadows School of the Arts Faculty Development Grant Program.

Introduction

When the events of September 11, 2001, unfolded, I was shocked and horrified, like all Americans, but I wasn't totally surprised. I had just finished two summers of teaching in Uzbekistan and Kazakhstan. Both countries, predominantly Muslim, are geographically and culturally situated near Afghanistan, where the terrorists were trained.

A grant from the U.S. Department of State funded my trips. I stayed in the homes of local residents, taught at local universities, and spent many hours talking to college students about their lives and their concerns. Most were not optimistic about the future. Their countries were plagued with problems, including a lack of jobs, a weak economy, militant Islamist movements, corruption in government, poor living conditions and oppressive dictatorial leadership.

Hardline Muslim fundamentalists had taught many of these young people to despise America. The plight of the Palestinians and America's support for Israel also fueled the fires of hatred. But what could I, as a professor of advertising, do about it?

In late 2001, I heard that one of the world's most accomplished advertising executives, Charlotte Beers, was preparing an advertising campaign about the United States for the Arab and Muslim world. I had known of Beers since I began to study and work in advertising about 20 years ago.

So when my friend and research partner, Alice Kendrick, phoned me in early December 2002 and invited me to come to Dallas and hear Beers speak at Southern Methodist University, I knew it was an opportunity I couldn't pass up. Alice and I had been following Beers' activities since she had joined the State Department as Under Secretary of State for Public Diplomacy and Public Affairs.

Before the visit, Alice and I obtained a copy of the television commercials Beers had produced that were airing in the Middle East. We read about the "Shared Values Initiative" (SVI) campaign and began formulating a program of research to study it. We were fascinated with, but skeptical of, the idea that the government could use consumer advertising techniques to sell America to citizens of other countries.

We met Beers for the first time at her hotel in Fort Worth and drove her to SMU, where she explained the purpose of SVI to students, faculty and Dallas business and civic leaders. We told Beers about our interest in the SVI campaign and our desire to examine its effectiveness. She said the advertising phase of SVI was coming to an end and, therefore, there wasn't enough time to put a study together.

However, Beers said she believed the campaign was effective, despite its critics. The campaign had achieved its main goal, she said, which was to start a dialogue with audiences in the Arab and Muslim world. She wanted to make ordinary Muslim citizens aware that America wasn't such a bad place. Even if they thought the ads were propaganda, Beers said, the ads made them think and got them talking.

At SMU, Beers gave an ad agency-style multimedia presentation that included clips of Secretary of State Colin L. Powell on an MTV call-in talk show speaking with young people from around the world. She answered questions from the audience but avoided discussing U.S./Middle East foreign policy issues. In fact, she told one particularly irritated political science professor, "If you have problems with the policy, talk to your Congressman. My job is simply to communicate the policy in the most favorable light possible." It reminded me of the role of advertising executives. They don't make the product; they simply sell it.

A few weeks later we learned from news reports that the SVI ads had stopped running. A few months later we learned that Beers was leaving the State Department for "medical reasons."

The end of the SVI television spots and Beers' resignation did not dampen our interest in studying the campaign. SVI represented a first-of-its-kind use of advertising, and it appeared that very little research had been conducted to measure its effectiveness.

In the summer of 2003, with funding from a small university grant, Alice and I traveled to London to conduct research on the SVI commercials. We employed an experimental research design and showed the SVI spots to international students who rated their effectiveness, believability and credibility. We were surprised by the results: After viewing the commercials, the students had more favorable opinions of the United States.

Later, with the help of graduate students, we replicated the experiment in other countries with the same results. Armed with our data, we went home and wrote three academic conference papers on the campaign and its effectiveness. Our research was well received in the academic community and caught the attention of communication scholars at the University of Michigan.

In October 2003, the Yaffe Center at the University of Michigan organized a small workshop around the topic of "communicating with skeptical audiences." State Department officials were invited to Ann Arbor to meet over a three-day period with academic and professional communicators from across the country—all experts in the field of persuasive communication and public diplomacy. Alice and I were invited to share our findings pertaining to the Shared Values Initiative.

State Department officials were skeptical about our research. That didn't surprise me. But I was surprised to learn that these seasoned bureaucrats had relatively little knowledge about communication processes and research. These were the people our country entrusted with the responsibility of communicating America's message to the outside world, but they appeared to know very little about communication or marketing.

When it came time to present our research on the Shared Values Initiative, the State Department representatives were dismissive even before we began. One said, "Charlotte is gone and we are never doing that again." Like so many others, they had assumed the campaign was a failure.

We knew then that we had to write this book. We needed to document the story of the Shared Values Initiative for students, professional communicators, public policy makers and scholars. We needed to let people know that the idea of using advertising-based communication and other modern marketing techniques might be an appropriate and effective strategy in the war on terrorism after all.

But the bureaucrats at the State Department didn't make our job any easier. They repeatedly denied our requests for public records and other materials and refused to allow the executives at McCann-Erickson, the advertising agency that created the controversial commercials, to speak with us.

Fortunately, Beers and others gave us copies of many of the internal State Department documents related to SVI. The story of SVI is built largely from these documents and from interviews with Beers and other officials, as well as from news stories and broadcast news programs. This book also contains reviews of the literature on public diplomacy, propaganda, advertising effects, theories of persuasion and, of course, our own original research.

More specifically:

- The first chapter of this book chronicles the SVI campaign.
- Chapter 2 provides an historical examination of SVI by exploring the history of public diplomacy and propaganda since WWI.
- The third chapter reviews other elements of SVI, including radio and newspaper components and other public diplomacy programs that were part of Beers' tenure at the State Department.

- Chapter 4 analyzes the negative reactions to SVI by the international and domestic media, the State Department, Congress, the advertising industry and scholars.
- In Chapter 5, we present the principles of persuasive communication and explain measures of advertising effectiveness.
- Chapter 6 reviews our experimental research, which suggests that the SVI commercials could have been successful in favorably changing attitude toward America.
- And in the final chapter, we provide observations about SVI and recommendations for communicating with Arab and Muslim audiences in the future.

Readers may view the actual SVI commercials by visiting <www.osu-tulsa.okstate.edu/sharedvalues>. We suggest that readers watch the SVI commercials on our Web site now before reading the rest of this book.

We know that even after reading this book some people will be skeptical of our research findings and our general premise—that advertising may be useful as a tool in public diplomacy. But, like Beers, we believe that opening a dialogue and getting people to think is a first step. Only through better communication and mutual understanding can our country hope to win the war on terrorism.

—Jami Fullerton, associate professor of advertising,
Oklahoma State University, Winter 2006

"We've got to get creative people from
the most creative media society on the face of the earth
to put their time, attention and mind power to this."

———————————————

Colin L. Powell, Secretary of State,
before the Senate Foreign Relations Committee
October 25, 2001

Chapter 1

A Brief History of the Shared Values Initiative

Shortly after the September 11th attacks, former advertising executive Charlotte Beers, an under secretary in the U.S. Department of State, purchased $5 million of commercial airtime on Middle Eastern and Asian television stations. The goal of the Shared Values Initiative was to convince the Arab and Muslim world that America wasn't waging war on Islam. The Madison Avenue produced ads depicted the happy lives of Muslims in America, including Dr. Elias Zerhouni, director of the National Institutes of Health. This chapter recounts the Shared Values Initiative from the time Secretary of State Colin Powell decided to hire Beers until her resignation in March of 2003.

When Colin L. Powell took office as Secretary of State in January 2001, U.S. government spending on public diplomacy was at a low point. It had declined 50 percent in real dollars compared to the 1980s. America's chief international communication department, the United States Information Agency, had been disbanded and some of its functions absorbed by the U.S. Department of State.

Some government officials blamed the spending cuts on the fall of the Soviet Union and the end of Cold War. Public diplomacy— which can be defined as a government's effort to inform and influence the attitudes of the general public in a foreign country—had lost its importance in the post-Cold War world. As one State Department official put it: "[We thought] everybody would simply start watching American films and buying our products."[1]

Colin Powell when he was Secretary of State (Photo courtesy of the U.S. Department of State Web site)

Powell was obviously concerned about the lack of attention to public diplomacy. In March 2001, five months before 9/11, he told a House Budget Committee that the State Department would be "bringing people into the public diplomacy function of the department who are going to change from just selling us in the old USIA way to really branding foreign policy, branding the department, marketing the department, marketing American values to the world—and not just putting out pamphlets."[2]

And to sell "Brand America" to the world and especially to the Middle East, where America's image had suffered the most, he said he would be hiring a communication expert from the advertising industry. Her name was Charlotte Beers. She had served with him during the 1990s as a director on the board of Gulfstream Aerospace Corporation. She would become the second Under Secretary of State for Public Diplomacy and Public Affairs.

Beers, 66, who had just retired from the advertising business, seemed perfect for the job. She was one of the best advertising executives in America. Among other things, she held the honor of being the only person in history to have headed up two different top ten worldwide advertising agencies.

"When I heard Colin Powell talking about all that brand stuff," one Madison Avenue veteran told *New York Magazine*, "I thought, that came directly from Charlotte."[3]

Charlotte Beers

Beers was born in Beaumont, Texas, on July 26, 1935. Her father was a cowboy from Montana who ended up in the oil business. Her mother was a homemaker. She grew up in Lafayette, Louisiana, and Houston.

Charlotte Beers

After attending Baylor University and the University of Southwestern Louisiana, she graduated in 1957 with degrees in math and physics. She began working as a research supervisor at Uncle Ben's Rice in Houston, a division of Mars, Inc.

In 1966, Beers became one of the first female product brand managers for Uncle Ben's. In the 1970s, she became the first female senior vice president for J. Walter Thompson advertising.

In 1979, she joined Tatham Advertising and was named chief executive officer in 1982. She stayed at Tatham through the 1980s, quadrupling its business and spearheading its merger with RSCG advertising agency of Europe.

In 1988, she became the first woman in the 99-year history of the American Association of Advertising Agencies to be named chairman of the prestigious industry group. Beers left Tatham RSCG in 1991.

From 1992 to 1997, Beers served as Chairman and CEO of Ogilvy & Mather. David Ogilvy later described her as someone with whom he had much in common. During her time at Ogilvy, she brought in new business—including the $900 million IBM account and $80 million in billings from Kentucky Fried Chicken—and reconnected with former Ogilvy blue-chip clients Shell, American Express and Ponds of Unilever. Beers' time at Ogilvy was written up as a Harvard Business School case study that continues to be taught in universities across the country.

At Ogilvy, Beers' approach was known as "brand stewardship," which she described as the art of creating, building and energizing profitable brands. She focused on taking "emotional ownership" of clients' brands and nurturing a relationship between the brand and the consumer.

Two years after retiring from Ogilvy, Beers took the helm of an advertising agency for the third time when she rejoined her former employer, J. Walter Thompson, as chairman of the board, agreeing to a two-year term. In 1999, the JWT management team brought in more than $700 million in new U.S. billings, which included Avon, Pepsi and KPMG.

As an advertising executive, Beers was admired for her energy, honesty, work ethic and flamboyant style. She once ate dog food at a campaign pitch for Mars pet products. On another occasion, she reassembled a power drill while making a formal presentation to executives at Sears. And during a debate with her client at Jaguar, she threw the keys to her own Jag on the conference table to emphasize the point that women can own a Jag, too. Her agency subsequently developed a television commercial featuring a woman driving a Jag while the Etta James' ballad "At Last My Love Has Come Along" played in the background.

As is the case with anyone who reaches the top, Beers also had her share of critics. She once was called the "Schmooze Queen of Madison Avenue," and some industry analysts and reporters have depicted her as a token female who used her southern charm to sway male clients. The trade press on occasion also made reference to what it called "Beers' beguiling manner."

But those who knew her best—her clients and coworkers—say she had a no-nonsense, honest approach to business. In 1992, *Glamour* magazine agreed, naming her "Woman of the Year" for breaking the glass ceiling in advertising. In 1996, *Fortune* magazine featured Beers on its cover—the first time a woman had ever appeared there. *Fortune* called Beers "the best—better than the men and all other women in the [advertising] business."[4]

On Oct. 2, 2001, Beers added another distinction to her list of accomplishments. She was sworn in as Under Secretary of State for Public Diplomacy and Public Affairs at the State Department.

Beers and the State Department

At the State Department, Beers was one of six Under Secretaries who reported to Powell. His primary job was to advance the President's foreign policy.

Her predecessor was Evelyn Lieberman, whose previous assignment at the White House was to keep Monica Lewinsky and President Clinton separated. When Lieberman was transferred to the Under Secretary position, she was considered a "place holder" until the Bush administration could make an appointment.

Beers was in charge of the public diplomacy section, whose communication efforts are aimed at informing and influencing an international audience. She supervised the Bureau of Public Affairs, the Bureau of Educational and Cultural Affairs, and the Office of International Information Programs.

The Bureau of Public Affairs was responsible for communicating U.S. foreign policy to Americans through press briefings, town meetings and the State Department Web site. The Bureau of Educational and Cultural Affairs coordinated cultural and professional exchanges abroad. And the Office of International Information Programs, through which the Shared Values Initiative (SVI) was launched, served as the principal international communications service.

Beers quickly became known as one of "Powell's People," which distinguished her from career bureaucrats and from Bush appointees. But the link to Powell didn't necessarily make her job any easier. State Department bureaucrats, like government bureaucrats in general, often resent outsiders, and they didn't spare Beers from any of this resentment.

Reaction to Beers' Appointment

The events of 9/11 elevated the importance of public diplomacy. President George W. Bush himself echoed this point on September 20, 2001, when he appeared before a joint session of Congress and rhetorically asked, "Why do they hate us?"[5]

But not everyone was pleased with Powell's decision to hire Beers.

"We saw it as a bold and interesting appointment," an unnamed State Department diplomat told *New York Magazine*.[6] "I mean, I like Charlotte very much, but her appointment was preposterous."

Advertising Age also pointed out that "not all marriages of business people and government succeed."[7]

Responding to the critics, Powell said Beers "got me to buy Uncle Ben's rice, so what's wrong with getting somebody who knows how to sell something?" He also pointed out that "we (the State Department) are selling a product. We need someone who can rebrand American foreign policy, rebrand American diplomacy."[8]

Powell clearly had confidence in Beers' abilities. But his defense of Beers didn't mollify those who were critical of the rebranding idea itself. As William Drake of the Carnegie Endowment for International Peace put it: "I just find the notion that you can sell Uncle Sam like Uncle Ben's [rice] highly problematic."[9]

"You can't boil down America into a slogan," added William Rugh, the president of America-Mideast Educational and Training Services, Inc., a nonprofit organization that promotes understanding between the United States and Middle East. "America isn't a single product—it's not Coca-Cola. If Charlotte Beers thinks America is a product to sell, that won't work."[10]

But the events of 9/11 usurped the criticism. Pressure was

mounting for the Bush administration to take a proactive role in combating terrorist propaganda and negative images of the United States in the Middle East.

In November 2001, *The New York Times* dubbed "Osama bin Laden a formidable propaganda foe" and declared that propaganda was "back in fashion" as a means of shaping public opinion.[11] Political pundits on Capitol Hill and at think tanks and universities across the nation also were calling on the Bush administration to employ public diplomacy as a weapon in the war on terrorism.

Beers and the Shared Values Initiative

No one needed to convince Charlotte Beers that "selling America" would be more difficult than selling rice.

On October 15, 2001, just two weeks after her confirmation, she told reporters at a meeting that "over time, we have to attempt to blunt and deflect the hate" that some Middle Easterners have for the United States.[12]

"You'll never communicate effectively unless you can walk in the shoes of your intended audience," she said. "That's a discipline you learn on day one in advertising work. And the communication we're about now is philosophical and psychological as well as factual. So we're in the position of having to speak to very distant, cynical—if not more hostile than that—audiences, and if we can't speak in their language, or start on some common ground, we're not going to have very effective communications."

In November 2001, she told the international press corps that "this is a tricky business" and "some efforts may backfire." But, she said, "consider the alternative, which is silence. We have no choice."[13]

"The whole idea of building a brand is to create a relationship between the product and its user," she said. "We're going to have to communicate the intangible assets of the United States—things like our belief system and our values."[14]

In an interview with NBC's Andrea Mitchell, Beers said she would attempt to "open a dialogue of mutual respect and understanding" with audiences overseas."[15] Internal State Department reports also show that Beers said the purpose of the "Shared Values Initiative" was "to foster free, candid and respectful engagement and exchange between Americans and people from the Muslim world."[16]

Developing the Shared Values Initiative

From the beginning, SVI was known as "Charlotte's project," according to one long-time State Department staffer. State Department Press Secretary Richard Boucher acknowledged that Beers had full control of the project and final approval of the ads.[17]

While Beers had extensive experience in branding, marketing and mass communication, she had little experience as a bureaucrat or diplomat. In terms of politics, no one knew on which side she fell. Some of the State Department staffers viewed her as "this weird couture-wearing woman who spoke from the hip." Apparently these two things—wearing trendy clothing and speaking what is on one's mind—didn't play out well in bureaucratic Washington.

Despite clashes with State Department staff and the diplomatic corps, Beers remained determined to develop a campaign that would improve America's image abroad.

She spent much of her time explaining her goals to others. Many of her presentations resembled a college introductory course in communications, which usually includes graphic presentations of the classic sender-message-receiver communication model. Basic instructions on how persuasion and advertising worked became a staple of her interaction with the public and government.

In interviews and presentations, she made it clear that her goal was to reach the people of the Arab and Muslim world with messages that emphasized the humanity and tolerance of the American people.

According to Beers, the ultimate goal for the campaign would be "discussion and debate," as opposed to changing minds about U.S. foreign policy.

She believed the primary target audience for SVI was "the people." Specifically Beers cited the importance of reaching women in the target countries—"the mothers and teachers."

To accomplish that task, she would harness the power of mainstream media, especially television. The messages would be "from the people and to the people" as opposed to "from government-to-government" or "from elite-to-elite"—the way most public diplomacy efforts had been managed in the past and the style preferred by most U.S. ambassadors.

Beers was systematic in her approach. To better understand people of the Middle East, she consulted the RoperASW Worldwide research tool known as ValueScope™, which employs on-going international consumer research about "core belief systems based on personal values."

ValueScope™ identifies 57 discrete values that exist throughout the world. Respondents randomly selected from 35 countries are asked to rank the values, which are printed on separate cards, that are most important to them. Respondents first divide the cards into three piles—"most important values to me," "somewhat important values to me" and "values not important to me." Respondents then sort the cards within each stack so that values are arranged from most to least important. These rankings are combined to provide a composite ranking of values for each country.

The 2002 ValueScope™ data showed vast differences between the United States and Muslim countries such as Saudi Arabia and Indonesia on values such as modesty, obedience, duty, perseverance and freedom. The same research revealed significant agreement among people of predominantly Muslim nations and the United States regarding the values of faith, family and learning.

Based on these findings, Beers designed a campaign to focus on

Table 1.1
U.S. and Selected Countries
Compared in Terms of Values
(Smallest Number=Most Important Value)

"Some of our ratings are far apart."

Value	United States	Saudi Arabia	
Modesty	40	6	
Obedience	36	10	
Freedom	3	25	
	United States	Indonesia	
Duty	31	6	
Perseverance	76	7	
Freedom	3	37	

"But very significant other values are held in common."

	United States	Saudi Arabia	Indonesia
Faith	5	1	1
Family	1	3	3
Learning	6	4	8

Source: Data and quoted material from Charlotte Beers' presentation on the Shared Values Initiative.

the common interests or "Shared Values" of Americans and Muslims—namely family, religion and education.

The data in Table 1.1 and accompanying quotes are taken

directly from a Beers' presentation given at Southern Methodist University on December 5, 2002, to an audience of students, faculty and civic leaders in Dallas. Compiled from a Roper ValueScope™ January 2002 study of 35 countries, they show that people in Saudi Arabia and Indonesia place more value on modesty, obedience, duty and perseverance than people in the United States. In contrast, people in the United States place more value on freedom. However, all three countries place a great deal of value on faith, family and learning.

Like other advertising professionals, Beers assumed that advertising campaigns cannot accomplish multiple objectives. So the key issue on which she focused was religious tolerance.

Polls had shown that many Muslims viewed Americans as decadent and irreligious. Beers also knew that the Islamic faith was the fastest growing religion in America. Thus, the SVI spots would be designed to show American Muslims freely practicing their faith, teaching their children the Koran and following the "straight path."

The decision to stress religion may have indirectly affected the outcome of the campaign. Production and airing of the television commercials was delayed four months because U.S. Justice Department lawyers were worried that the Islamic content in the commercials could violate the legal separation between church and state. The commercials were re-shot and edited to remove verbal references to "Allah," which were sprinkled throughout the on-air dialogue.

State Department officials and others associated with the campaign regretted that the spots were not broadcast before global publicity began swirling about the impending war in Iraq (March 2003) and the U.S. government's crackdown on identifying and tracking Muslims living in the United States. In fall 2003, a Congressional report issued by a bi-partisan advisory panel on public diplomacy led by former Ambassador Edward Djerejian, known as the Djerejian Report, cited the extensive time required for producing the spots as one of several shortcomings of SVI (see Chapter 4 for more details).

Asked later if she would have done anything differently, Beers mentioned the "legal clearance" issue. But she added that the delay was not a major problem because it allowed for the airing of the spots during the season of Ramadan, a month of fasting and reflection similar to Lent in the Christian tradition. Beers never regretted using religious tolerance as the key message of the campaign.

The Council of American Muslims for Understanding

A key problem confronting Beers and the SVI team was sponsorship. If the U.S. Department of State was identified as the source of the commercials, then viewers might see them as propaganda, and, hence, the credibility of the entire campaign could suffer.

So in the spring of 2002, Beers and the State Department asked Malik Hasan, a Muslim Republican-leaning retired medical executive, for help in creating a nonprofit, nonpartisan organization called The Council of American Muslims for Understanding (CAMU).

At a press conference in May 2002, Beers said the organization would be "dedicated to providing a better understanding of Islam in America to the people in the United States and throughout the world."[18]

Needless to say, some critics complained that CAMU was really a front for the State Department, and that it was inappropriately or illegally created or funded. Hasan denied those charges and argued that although CAMU is government funded, it's not government founded.[19]

He said the State Department had given grant money to CAMU to spread the message of religious tolerance in America to people overseas. But he said the State Department did not play a significant role in the development of CAMU's mission statement.

Some Christian religious leaders in the United States also criticized the arrangement, saying the U.S. government showed favoritism to the Islamic religion.[20] Others questioned the constitutionality of the relationship, arguing that the State Department may have violated the principle of the separation of church and state.

Beers said the State Department sought input from members of CAMU when it created the SVI program. She also said CAMU was indispensable in helping the State Department develop a more positive dialogue with some of the Islamic countries.

Undoubtedly, attribution of the advertisements to the Council of American Muslims for Understanding was a strategic decision designed to enhance source credibility and make the message more believable. The final seconds of the SVI commercials also identify "the American people" as a cosponsor of the advertisement, even though most Americans knew nothing of the campaign. Beers' choice to invoke U.S. people rather than the U.S. government also was, no doubt, designed to steer attention away from the State Department's role in the project.

In October 2002, the State Department launched SVI. The campaign included speeches by diplomats and American Muslims to international audiences, "town hall" events in several countries, Internet sites and chat rooms, a 60-page four-color magazine titled *Muslim Life in America*, a series of newspaper ads and five television commercials/advertisements.

The commercials—or "mini-documentaries" as the State Department preferred to call them—were the most important component of SVI (see Table 1.2 and Appendix A). All components of the SVI campaign were produced in English and various Middle Eastern languages and dialects such as Arabic, Farsi and Urdu.

In one of the SVI commercials, American Muslim Dr. E. Zerhouni, director of the National Institutes of Health, shakes hands with President Bush and is thanked for his outstanding contribution to medicine. See Table 1.2 for more details.

McCann-Erickson Produces Spots

Beers hired advertising agency McCann-Erickson to produce the Shared Values Initiative commercials and buy the media time and space in the targeted countries using $15 million of the $595 million State Department budget. Although criticized as being excessive, $15 million for an international branding campaign is a relatively small amount.

McCann-Erickson was chosen because it was one of the few

Table 1.2
The Five Television Commercials

The central component of the Shared Values Initiative was five television commercials produced for broadcasting over Middle Eastern television stations. A "slice-of-life" format was used. Each contained a testimonial, which showed happy, prosperous American Muslims in various personal and professional roles. All of the spots featured actual American Muslims actively practicing their religion and commenting positively on the tolerance Americans have for the Muslim faith. A brief description of each is below. The complete storyboards are contained in Appendix A. The ads also can be viewed at <www.osu-tulsa.okstate.edu/sharedvalues>.

- "Baker" profiles an average day in a busy family-run bakery/restaurant in Toledo, Ohio, owned by an American-Muslim family. The commercial highlights the interaction between the Muslim owners and their non-Muslim American clientele.
- "Doctor" showcases the accomplishments of Dr. Elias Zerhouni, whom President George W. Bush had named as Director of the National Institutes of Health. Dr. Zerhouni, born in Algeria, describes his life as a successful government official and respected American Muslim. During the spot, Dr. Zerhouni is shown shaking hands and speaking with President Bush.
- "School Teacher" features Rawai Ismail working as a public school teacher in Toledo, Ohio. The spot shows her wearing a hijab while teaching elementary school children and later holding Saturday Koran classes in her home.
- "Journalist" follows an Indonesian journalism student at the University of Missouri through a typical day as a reporter for the school's television newscast, as a college student and as a practicing Muslim.
- "Firefighter" focuses on two New York City employees: a young firefighter who shares his experiences since September 11th and a chaplain who explains how he helps city employees. In the spot, the young firefighter describes the closeness he feels to both his Muslim and non-Muslim coworkers and the neighborhood.

At the end of the commercials, the viewer is presented with the line, "Presented by the Council of American Muslims for Understanding." The frame then dissolves to a final frame of solid black and the words, "And the American People."

large global advertising agencies that had no business or financial connections to Beers.

The agency's executives refused requests for interviews because the State Department, their client, refused to give them permission to talk with us. However, according to State Department documents and individuals involved first-hand in the project, McCann-Erickson created the spots under Beers' guidance. CAMU and other advertising consultants also assisted in the production process.

The American Muslims appearing in the spots were not professional actors but were real people who had been chosen after a series of interviews. According to a State Department employee who worked on the commercial production, "We didn't pay them. We didn't script them. We just filmed them in their daily lives."

The SVI Television Campaign

The SVI television campaign began airing October 29, 2002, in Indonesia, which is the largest Muslim nation in the world. Eighty percent of its 220 million people are Muslim. The campaign was then broadcast in what the State Department described as a "sequential rollout" to other Muslim countries.

The State Department initially hoped to get free airtime in the Islamic countries. However, all of the targeted countries, except the former Soviet republics of Kazakhstan and Azerbaijan, refused to run the spots at no charge. At this point, the State Department decided to purchase airtime on international TV stations; however, most countries still refused to broadcast the spots on their state-owned system—even U.S.-friendly countries such as Egypt and Jordan.

Al-Jazeera, the pan-Arab television station sometimes referred to as "the CNN of the Arab World," initially said it would consider it "an honor" to accept the U.S. message but later refused to air the spots. State Department spokesperson Richard Boucher said at a press briefing that Al-Jazeera "wanted too much money."[21]

Under Secretary of State for Public Diplomacy and Public Affairs Charlotte Beers in her State Department office.

As such, only about $5 million of the total $15 million budgeted for the advertising was spent. On PBS's "NewsHour with Jim Lehrer," Beers said the governments probably refused to run the SVI spots because they considered the ads "propaganda."[22]

The spots did air on a number of state-run media systems in Pakistan, Malaysia, Indonesia and Kuwait. Viewers in other countries, such as Jordan, Egypt, Saudi Arabia, Bahrain, Oman, Qatar, Lebanon and the United Arab Emirates, also saw the commercials via pan-Arab satellite.[23]

The SVI spots ran in Kenya and Tanzania through embassy placement.[24] Other embassy placements were not secured, possibly due in many cases to lack of "ambassador buy-in." One State Department employee involved in the SVI campaign acknowledged that most of the U.S. ambassadors in the targeted countries were not supportive of the SVI campaign and, therefore, did not encourage the host country to run the spots.

Some officials close to Beers and the campaign have speculated that the ambassadors' opposition to the SVI campaign may have been the primary reason that the SVI spots received limited airtime and distribution, although news reporters covering the story never followed up on this theory. Beers later privately admitted that embassy buy-in was one of the areas she should have focused on.

Conflicting Reports

The SVI television campaign was discontinued in early December 2002. But the reasons why are not entirely clear.

McCann's media flowcharts and internal State Department documents indicate that SVI commercials were scheduled to run only through early December 2002. However, on January 16, 2003, *The Wall Street Journal* wrote that SVI was discontinued by the State Department because it failed to register well with Muslim audiences and because many host governments refused to broadcast the commercials.

That same night Beers appeared on CNN and told anchor Aaron Brown that the campaign had not been suspended and would continue. She said that the television spots were modified slightly for extended use beyond Ramadan and were running in countries throughout "Africa and Central Asia, both through paid and free placements."[25]

On February 3, 2003, the State Department said that the spots had stopped running in December, as planned, and that they would be revised to remove mentions of Ramadan before airing again. They never aired again (see Table 1.3 for time line).

Reactions to the Commercials

Immediately after the "mini-documentaries" aired in late October 2002, U.S. media began reporting that the campaign was not

Table 1.3
Time Line for Shared Values Initiative

Early 2001
Colin Powell asks Charlotte Beers to be Under Secretary of Public Diplomacy and Public Affairs for George W. Bush.

Sept. 11, 2001
Terrorists attack the World Trade Center and the Pentagon.

Oct. 2, 2001
Charlotte Beers is sworn in and charged with the task of "selling America's core values to the Muslim world."

May 2002
The State Department forms the Council of American Muslims for Understanding (CAMU).

Oct. 28, 2002 to Dec. 8, 2002
Television ad campaign runs in Indonesia, Malaysia, Pakistan, Kuwait and on pan-Arab satellite.   Al-Jazeera Television and key Arab countries refuse to run the spots.

Jan. 16, 2003
The Wall Street Journal reports that the campaign was suspended because it failed. Beers tells CNN that campaign would continue.

Feb. 3, 2003
The State Department reports that ads stopped running in December and were being revised.

March 3, 2003
Beers resigns for "health reasons."

After March 2003
Media, Congress, industry and administration criticize SVI and distance themselves from Beers.

well received.

The chief complaint by those who viewed the spots in the targeted countries was that they did not explain U.S. foreign policy.

One Jakarta cab driver was quoted as saying, "I don't know what the point is."[26]

The international media were even more critical, with one Malaysian newspaper calling the campaign a "waste of time" and one Pakistani newspaper labeling it "another Zionist propaganda tool."[27]

A London-based Saudi commentator said that the campaign caused incitement against U.S. policy in several Islamic countries, including demonstrations denouncing U.S. policy in Indonesia.[28]

American Muslim and university professor Mamoun Fandy told PBS that the campaign had "contributed to anti-Americanism in the region."[29]

Some foreign news media were less critical. Pan-Arab newspaper *Al Hayat* said the campaign was justified because American society was composed of different cultures and ethnic groups. Other news sources applauded the U.S. government for acknowledging that it had a tarnished image in the Arab world. Chapter 4 explores reactions to SVI in more depth.

The State Department was frequently asked how the effects of the campaign could be measured, but it failed to produce any formal evaluation. State Department spokesman Richard Boucher said the plan was to "gauge initial reaction from the newspapers, people we talk to, statements that are made and just [by] trying to get an idea of how it's playing as we go forward."[30]

According to Beers, any and all responses to the campaign would be considered good—and "the more negative the response from the underground powers in the Muslim world, the more effective the campaign."

She told CNN that the campaign would be successful if it started a dialogue "about things which we have in common." According to Beers, people who saw the spots in other countries were surprised that the United States had mosques and that a teacher could work with her head covered. She did not reveal the source of this information.

Research conducted by McCann-Erickson also showed positive reactions to SVI. This information was presented to Congress February 27, 2003, during a hearing on American Public Diplomacy and Islam.

Beers reported to the Senate Committee on Foreign Relations that SVI messages were seen by 288 million people throughout the Arab and Muslim world and that, according to McCann-Erickson research in Indonesia, SVI commercials scored higher on message recall and retention than those for "a typical soft drink

Charlotte Beers poses with Colin Powell after receiving the Distinguished Service Medal.

campaign run at higher spending levels for more months." But the U.S. press didn't give much publicity to this fact. More details of McCann-Erickson's post-campaign research can be found in Chapter 5.

During the same Congressional hearing, Beers defended SVI and explained her use of television as a way to reach the ordinary people who may have believed that Muslims in America are treated harshly. She told the committee that randomly taped interviews with people on the street in Indonesia clearly revealed that the SVI spots had opened their minds and challenged their beliefs.

Beers explained her future plans for SVI to the senators. She hoped to continue to use mass media and build on the Shared Values campaign with a new program called "Shared Futures." This program would bring sustained attention to economic, political and educational reform in the Muslim world, she said.

But Beers was never given the chance to launch the new media campaign or to defend SVI further. In March 2003, she resigned, citing health reasons.

The French newspaper *Le Monde* speculated that her resignation was brought on by the enormous difficulties of communicating the U.S. message overseas.[31]

O'Dwyer's PR Web site celebrated her departure, saying "Good riddance!" and "About time! She was horrible and the U.S. has lost all post-9/11 support."[32]

Marketing Week's lead headline announced "Beers bombs in the Middle East."[33]

Colin Powell ignored the critics. Before Beers left office, he awarded her with the State Department's highest honor—the Distinguished Service Medal.

Chapter Endnotes

[1]Dan Gilgoff and Jay Tolson, "Losing friends? The departure of a top U.S. diplomat renews questions about how to fight anti-Americanism," *U.S. News & World Report*, 17 March 2003, p. 40.

[2]House Budget Committee, "U.S. Representative Jim Nussle (R-IA) holds hearing on State Department fiscal year 2002 budget priorities," 15 March 2001. Retrieved from FDCH Political Transcripts on LexisNexis.

[3]Simon Dumenco, "Stopping spin Laden," *New York Magazine*, 12 November 2001. Retrieved from http://newyorkmetro.com/nymetro/news/media/features/5379/.

[4]Patricia Sellers, "Women, sex and power," *Fortune*, 5 August 1996, p. 42.

[5]George Walker Bush, "Address before a joint session of the Congress on the United States response to the terrorist attacks of September 11," September 2001. Washington, D.C.: Weekly Compilation of Presidential Documents. Retrieved March 15, 2004, from ProQuest database.

[6]Dumenco, "Stopping spin Laden."

[7]"Diplomat Beers," *Advertising Age*, 1 October 2001, p. 16.

[8]"From Uncle Ben's to Uncle Sam; Face value," *The Economist*, 23 February 2002, p. 96.

[9]Alexandra Starr, "Charlotte Beers' toughest sell: Can she market America to hostile Muslims abroad?" *Business Week*, 17 December 2001, p. 56.

[10]Dumenco, "Stopping spin Laden."

[11]Elizabeth Becker, "In the war on terrorism, a battle to shape opinion," *The New York Times,* 11 November 2001, p. A1.

[12]Robert G. Kaiser, "U.S. message lost overseas: Officials see immediate need for 'public diplomacy,'" *The Washington Post,* 15 October 2001, p. A1.

[13]Starr, "Charlotte Beers' toughest sell," p. 58.

[14]Starr, "Charlotte Beers' toughest sell."

[15]Andrea Mitchell, "Bush hires advertising executive to pour out PR messages over Afghanistan," NBC Nightly News, 7 November 2001. Transcript retrieved from http://www.prfirms.org/resources/news/bush_hires_110701.asp on 10 November 2005.

[16]Internal State Department documents, "Shared Values Initiative program rationale."

[17]State Department Daily Press Briefing, Richard Boucher, Spokesman, 30 October 2002. Retrieved from http://www.state.gov/r/pa/prs/dpb/2002/14805.htm on 1 November 2005.

[18]From the State Department's Open Dialogue Web site under *About This Partnership.* Retrieved from http://www.opendialogue.com/english/about.html on March 25, 2003.

[19]Mark O'Keefe, "U.S. gives money to Muslim group to help image," *Christian Century,* 5 June 2002, p. 17.

[20]Ibid.

[21]State Department Daily Press Briefing, Richard Boucher, Spokesman, 30 October 2002. Retrieved from http://www.state.gov/r/pa/prs/dpb/2002/14805.htm on 1 November 2005.

[22]"Public Diplomacy," Online NewsHour Transcript, 21 January 2003. Retrieved from www.pbs.org/newshour/media/public_diplomacy/beers_1-03.html on 18 April 2006.

[23]Pan-Arab satellite refers to television channels received via satellite by populations in multiple countries in the region and is not controlled by the government of a specific country.

[24]Ibid.

[25]State Department Daily Press Briefing, Richard Boucher, Spokesman, 30 October 2002. Retrieved from http://www.state.gov/r/pa/prs/dpb/2002/14805.htm on 1 November 2005.

[26]Atika Schubert, "U.S. tests charm offensive in Indonesia," CNN.com, 31 October 2002. Retrieved from http://edition.cnn.com/2002/WORLD/asiapcf/southeast/10/31/indonesia.us.campaign/ on 4 November 2005.

[27]Leslie Lau, "U.S. Muslim ad drive on Malaysian TV 'a waste of time,'" *Straits Times Singapore,* 6 November 2002. Retrieved from http://www.straitstimes.com.sg/asia on January 30, 2003.

[28]U.S. Department of State, Office of Research, "U.S. image in the Islamic world: Policy is the problem," Ben Goldberg (ed), 26 November 2002. Retrieved from http://www.globalsecurity.org/military/library/news/2002/11/mil-021126-wwwh21126.htm on 28 October 2003.

[29]"Public Diplomacy," *Online NewsHour* Transcript.

[30]State Department Daily Press Briefing, Richard Boucher, Spokesman, 30 October 2002. Retrieved from http://www.state.gov/r/pa/prs/dpb/2002/14805.htm on 1 November 2005

[31]Eric Leser, "The United States does not succeed in improving their image," *Le Monde,* 17 March 2003. Translated and retrieved from www.lemonde.fr on 18 March 2003.

[32]Center for Media and Democracy, "Charlotte Beers," *Source Watch* Retrieved from http://www.sourcewatch.org/index.php?title=Charlotte_Beers on 19 July 2004.

[33]"Beers Bombs in the Middle East," *Marketing Week*, 13 March 2003, p. 3.

Chapter 2

The Shared Values Initiative: Propaganda or Public Diplomacy?

Many scholars and government critics argue that there is no difference between public diplomacy and propaganda—they are both government-sponsored communication intended to persuade people that something is good or bad. Others, however, argue that propaganda is a form of mass communication that contains false or distorted information or ideas. This chapter examines various definitions of propaganda and provides a broad overview of U.S. public diplomacy from World War I through the Cold War. It concludes with an analysis of the Shared Values Initiative television campaign.

Even before the Shared Values Initiative (SVI) was launched, many critics were calling it "propaganda." This included not only Islamic radicals in some Muslim countries but also many journalists, scholars and politicians in America.

Although some scholars make no distinctions between propaganda and other persuasive content, most ordinary people do. The word "propaganda" evokes a plethora of negative images in the minds of most Americans, particularly the brainwashing experiments in Nazi Germany during World War II and Communist rhetoric during the Cold War. One of the easiest ways for powerful elites in a society to neutralize or destroy the persuasive potential of a message is to call it "propaganda."

Americans possess such a strong distaste for propaganda that Congress passed the Smith-Mundt Act in 1948 prohibiting the government from using propaganda against its own people. The Act banned domestic distribution of government-produced communication materials intended for consumption by overseas audiences.

Still in force today, Smith-Mundt provides the statutory authority for the State Department to disseminate information about U.S. policy and American society to international publics but not to Americans. That's why, for example, few Americans have heard a Voice of America radio broadcast or seen the SVI spots.

The Internet is breaking down some of these barriers. The Voice of America and the State Department both have Web sites (www.voanews.com and www.usinfo.state.gov) that provide content promoting U.S. policies and practices, and anyone with a link to the Internet can access them.

But would Americans call this content "propaganda?" Can propaganda be distinguished from public diplomacy messages and from content that government officials give to U.S. and international news media or make available to citizens via the mail, the Internet or live speeches? And what about the SVI campaign—was it public diplomacy or propaganda?

Defining Propaganda

The word propaganda is derived from the Latin *propagand,* which means "that which ought to be spread." The term originally was not intended to refer to misleading or false information. But today the word is almost always used pejoratively—to connote deceptive or distorted messages.

Origins of the Negative Connotation

The first two definitions of propaganda in *Webster's New World Dictionary* make no direct reference to this negative connotation: (a) "a committee of cardinals, the Congregation for the Propagation of the Faith, in charge of the foreign missions;" (b) "any systematic, widespread dissemination or promotion of particular ideas, doctrines, practices etc., to further one's own cause or to damage an opposing one." The third definition captures the meaning in its popular parlance: "ideas, doctrines, or allegations so spread: now often used disparagingly to connote deception or distortion."

The origins of the third definition are often traced to the so-called propaganda wars of World War I, when both sides created false and misleading posters, fliers and news reports to maintain morale at home and demoralize the enemy's armies and their peoples. In fact, in 1913, just before World War I, *Encyclopedia Britannica* did not even contain an entry for "propaganda," primarily because people did not use or understand the word.[1] The concept was virtually unknown outside of the Catholic Church.

Some evidence suggests that the negative connotation actually can be attributed to Pope Gregory XV and the Roman Catholic Church, which established in 1622 the *Sacra Congregatio de Propaganda Fide,* or the Propagation of Faith, to spread the Catholic faith to nonCatholic countries. To those within the Church, propaganda was virtually synonymous with education or teaching. It was the truth. However, the Cardinals who ran the propaganda office also were charged with combating Protestant ideas. So they produced materials that actively criticized the ideas and writings of the Protestants. Thus, to Protestants, "propaganda" referred to distorted, false or deceptive material.

Another possible source of the negative connotation was the Catholic Church's attacks on science and its defense of scholasticism—the doctrine that all knowledge came from the Bible (or God) and from the writings of classical philosophers, especially

Aristotle. Mass communication scholars Werner Severin and James Tankard suggest that propaganda picked up its association with untruths when the Catholic Church rejected scientific ideas,[2] most notably Copernicus' theory that the earth orbited the sun and Galileo's evidence to support that theory.

The second definition of propaganda in Webster's dictionary (see "b" above) is similar to the original Latin meaning and to popular definitions of persuasion because it doesn't assume the content is false or distorted. The emphasis, instead, is on dissemination of information and persuasion—on winning a battle of ideas.

Some mass communication scholars have picked up on this definition. Political scientist Harold Lasswell, whose work in the first half of the 20th century served as a foundation for much of the research and theory in the emerging discipline of mass communication, wrote a book based on his doctoral dissertation in 1927 on the use of propaganda during World War I. Lasswell's definition states that propaganda "refers solely to the control of opinion by significant symbols, or, to speak more concretely and less accurately, by stories, rumors, reports, pictures, and other forms of social communication.[3] Later, in 1937, Lasswell wrote a more precise definition of propaganda as "the technique of influencing human action by the manipulation of representations. These representations may take spoken, written, pictorial or musical form."[4]

Lasswell's definitions of propaganda point to the importance of symbols and imagery in communication, and some contemporary scholars focus more on this aspect of propaganda than on whether the communication contains false ideas. However, Lasswell's definitions are not widely used today because they are overly broad and may encompass any form of persuasive communication, including personal selling, advertising, publicity and possibly a parent encouraging a child toward some pro-social behavior.

The notion that propaganda involves distorted or false ideas and beliefs continues to dominate most conceptions of the term. For example, media scholars Stanley J. Baran and Dennis K. Davis also write that from the time of the Counter Reformation forward, propaganda has referred to "no-holds-barred use of communication to propagate specific beliefs and expectations."[5] And Barry Fulton, director of Public Diplomacy Institute at George Washington University, points out that after the mid-1960s propaganda took on "the tone of doing something underhanded."[6]

Contemporary communication scholars Garth Jowett and Victoria O'Donnell captured the idea when they defined propaganda as "the deliberate and systematic attempt to shape perceptions, manipulate cognitions, and direct behavior to achieve a response that furthers the desired intent of the propagandist."[7] In this definition, the use of the word "manipulate" implies that the creator of the message (propagandist) is deliberately attempting to control the person who is the object of the propaganda.

The Jowett and O'Donnell definition also draws attention to the two broad areas of mass communication research that have grown out of the study of propaganda. The first, attitude change, involves how messages can change predispositions, beliefs or feelings about an idea, product or person. The second, known as general effects, addresses the overall impact of mass communication messages on individuals and society.

These research areas are traditionally grounded in theories of persuasion and will be discussed in Chapter 5.

Black and White Propaganda

Many contemporary scholars also distinguish between two and sometimes three types of propaganda. The first is "black propaganda," which is associated with deception, misinformation and outright lies. Black propaganda would include coercive, aggressive and non-objective communication, which may be completely false, such as a government's dissemination of fabricated stories of enemy atrocities during wartime.

The second type is "white propaganda," which involves selective use of the truth, or the promotion of positive and the suppression of negative information. An example of this would include a government official's explanation and defense of his or her country's foreign policy. Advertising could also qualify as white propaganda.

The third type of propaganda is "gray," which involves a blending of the first two—factual statements "framed" or "spun" in such a way to distort their meaning, which is a popular technique among political commentators.

Although definitions that distinguish between false ideas and selective use of the truth are certainly useful, one problem with the conceptualization of white propaganda is that all mass-mediated communication could qualify for that designation. That's because no communication can account for all aspects or elements of a phenomenon. It can never tell the "whole truth." Something is always left out, because time and space in mass media are finite.

Moreover, there is also the problem of determining how much content is necessary to disqualify a message from the label "white propaganda." For example, if a governmental program has 99 so-called "positive effects" and one "negative effect" and if a truth-based message about the program emphasizes only the positive effects, should the message be called white propaganda? In other words, how much lack of emphasis on the so-called negative aspects of a phenomenon qualifies a communication for the label of "white propaganda?"

Because most people think of propaganda as deliberate attempts to distort or falsify, the white propaganda designation may stigmatize all forms of communication, even those that contain truth-statements. Consequently, some scholars prefer a more narrow definition of propaganda—one that limits that designation to false or distorted ideas.[8]

Propaganda or Persuasion?

The concepts of propaganda and persuasion are closely linked, and both refer to communication strategies that seek to change the receiver's attitude in favor of the sender's position. In distinguishing propaganda from persuasion, it may be useful to think about black versus white propaganda as described above. Black propaganda, characterized by lies and deception, may be what is now generally called propaganda. White propaganda, with its emphasis on the positive, might be considered persuasion.

Jowett and O'Donnell's definition makes the important distinction between persuasion and propaganda and is, therefore, more useful than earlier definitions. The idea that the propagandist's goal is to persuade the receiver to the advantage of the propagandist *but not necessarily to the benefit of the receiver* is a key factor differentiating propaganda from persuasion. Under this definition, propagandists will use whatever means they have available to persuade the audience to believe their argument, even if they must resort to exaggeration, omission or outright lies.

Jowett distinguished propaganda from persuasion when he wrote that propaganda is "deliberately planned, usually highly organized, and almost never ad hoc."[9] The propaganda efforts of Joseph Goebbels in Nazi Germany during the 1930s and of the Soviets during the Cold War are examples that fit Jowett's definition of propaganda.

Some people also may argue that contemporary "media spin" from politicians, pundits and commentators qualifies as propaganda under this definition. They contend that the message is planned by a sophisticated organization and may be interpreted as one-sided, if not blatantly deceptive, and definitely self-serving.

Others say that advertising is propaganda because it is an organized effort to convince people to buy products that they may not need. However, advertising—if deserving of the propaganda label—might qualify as white propaganda because it accentuates the positive while omitting the negative. Still others see advertising as simply a form of persuasive communication.

Richard Nelson, author of *A Chronology and Glossary of Propaganda in the United States*, says the difference between propaganda and persuasion is whether mass media are used in disseminating the message. According to Nelson, propaganda uses mass media whereas persuasion may be mass-mediated or interpersonal.

Thus, according to Nelson, propaganda is neutrally defined as a systematic form of persuasion which attempts to influence the emotions, attitudes, opinions, and actions of specified target audiences for ideological, political or commercial purposes through the controlled transmission of one-sided messages (which may or may not be factual) via mass and direct media channels. A propaganda organization is one that employs people who engage in propagandism—the applied creation and distribution of such forms of persuasion.[10]

What Is Public Diplomacy?

If we accept Webster's third, more popular definition of propaganda, then numerous examples of propaganda exist in society. But does all public diplomacy content then qualify as propaganda?

The *Encyclopedia Britannica* defines "diplomacy" as the "established method of influencing the decisions and behavior of foreign governments and peoples through dialogue, negotiation, and other measures short of war or violence."[11] Diplomacy is a critical part of foreign policy and international relations as countries seek to promote their interests globally and otherwise peacefully co-exist.

In modern times, diplomacy has taken two forms: (1) traditional diplomacy, which is characterized by interaction and communication among government leaders, (2) and public diplomacy, a government's effort to influence the attitudes of the general public in a foreign country.[12]

Traditional diplomacy is carried out by government leaders privately communicating with their foreign counterparts in a primarily secretive manner, while public diplomacy is open communication with citizens of other countries through various channels, including printed materials, student exchanges, public lectures and global press conferences. As former Under Secretary of State Charlotte Beers explained at a Congressional sub-committee hearing on public diplomacy in August 2004, public diplomacy is people-to-people while traditional diplomacy is elite-to-elite. According to Beers, both types of diplomacy are important in advancing America's interests abroad.

Public diplomacy is generally used to describe the official public communication efforts of the American government with audiences abroad. The State Department is now the central organization for public diplomacy functions. Its activities include the dissemination of information about U.S. policy and society to foreign audiences under the Smith-Mundt Act and cultural and education exchanges between Americans and foreign nationals under the Fulbright-Hayes Act.

State Department public affairs personnel, working in Washington and in U.S. embassies and offices overseas, translate and disseminate messages related to the United States throughout the world. Information officers use a variety of tactics to communicate American policies and culture to international audiences. These include issuing press releases to foreign media, providing pamphlets and other printed materials to citizens of other countries, maintaining a pro-U.S. Web site and operating reading rooms in international cities. Information officers are charged with telling "America's story to the world"—the motto of the United States Information Agency (USIA) before it was folded into the State Department.

In this respect, the State Department is similar to a public relations department at a major corporation. It works to control information about the organization and to favorably influence public attitudes. As Leo Bogart said in his study of the USIA: "A great power must communicate" and project a positive image overseas.[13]

Is Public Diplomacy Propaganda?

If one employs Webster's second, less sinister definition of propaganda, then clearly there would be no difference between public diplomacy and propaganda. Both involve dissemination of ideas and information. Many practitioners of public diplomacy readily call themselves propagandists and easily concede that public diplomacy is a substitute word for propaganda. Some scholars agree.

Nancy Snow, a communications professor and former USIA employee, writes in *Propaganda, Inc.*, that public diplomacy is a euphemism for propaganda.[14] She says the U.S. government prefers the term public diplomacy because "it doesn't want the American public to think that its own government engages in psychological warfare." Political scientists also use the terms "propaganda" and "public diplomacy" interchangeably to describe the communications activities of the government during wartime.[15]

However, if one uses Webster's third definition of propaganda, then the key issue is not who disseminates the ideas and information but whether the content distorts or falsifies. Although it would be incorrect to say the United States government has never distributed propaganda, it also would be incorrect to say that everything the government distributes is deceptive or untruthful. The content itself must be evaluated before such a label can be applied.

A Brief History of U.S. War Propaganda

Historical evidence shows that during times of war, all sides in a conflict produce false and distorted information and ideas. One of the most widely used devices is to overcount "enemy kills" and undercount a home country's losses in battle. For example, during the Revolutionary War and the Civil War, newspapers on both sides were guilty of this.

Propaganda and World War I

Modern propaganda in Europe began in the early 20th century when extremist political groups sought to form totalitarian governments. These totalitarian groups not only used military might to achieve control, they also simultaneously waged a communication war to convince the mass populations that their beliefs were right and good and all other beliefs were wrong and bad. These extremist groups used film and radio, two relatively new mass media technologies, to their political advantage.

As America was being drawn into World War I, President Woodrow Wilson was quick to recognize the power of propaganda in Europe, and in 1917 he launched the first large-scale U.S. government-sponsored communications agency, the Committee on Public Information (CPI). Wilson was cognizant of the connection of propaganda to Germany's cruel mass manipulation programs, so he chose to use "information" in the name of the committee rather than propaganda, although its mission included producing and distributing misleading messages to both foreign and domestic audiences.

CPI was also known as the Creel Committee—named after its chairman and Wilson's friend, George Creel, a well-known American journalist at the time. The duties of the Creel Committee included domestic communication objectives such as encouraging Americans to enlist in the military, buy war bonds and produce munitions. International objectives included boosting the morale of Allied countries, creating dissension in the Central Powers and "improving the American image abroad."[16]

Creel hired a cadre of talented communicators who used brilliant strategies to promote U.S. policy to Americans and the rest

George Creel (left) encouraged anti-German sentiments during World War I. He is shown here with Pop Warner, founder of Pop Warner football. (Photo courtesy of the *Los Gatos Weekly Times*)

of the world. Creel's propaganda programs were impressive, even in modern terms. They ranged from distributing millions of booklets about the reasons Americans were at war to patriotic speeches by influential speakers known as the "Four Minute Men" for their quick delivery. It was Creel who coined the phrase, "The War to End All Wars."[17]

Creel also effectively partnered with industry by urging Hollywood to produce and distribute pro-American movies. His committee leveraged the popularity of American movies among international theater owners by requiring the theaters to run pro-American short films prior to the main feature if they wished to show movies produced by the major Hollywood studios.

Creel's chief for Latin America, Edward Bernays, now known as the father of public relations (and also pejoratively as the "father of spin"), worked out a deal in which American companies that operated international retail outlets (e.g., Ford, Studebaker, Remington Typewriter and International Harvester) agreed to post pro-American posters in their shop windows. The same companies agreed to distribute pamphlets and sometimes withheld advertising from newspapers that criticized U.S. foreign policy.[18]

George Creel wrote about these programs and other activities of CPI in his book, *How We Advertised America: The First Telling of the Amazing Story of the Committee on Public Information that Carried the Gospel of Americanism to Every Corner of the Globe.*[19]

Smith-Mundt Act of 1948

At the end of World War I, America's propaganda machine slowed and the Creel Committee was disbanded. America turned inward.

While propaganda faded at home, it continued to ravage Europe as fascism and communism took hold, each wielding sophisticated, deceptive communication programs to gain power. There was no formal information agency in the United States between the World Wars, and President Franklin D. Roosevelt oversaw most of the communication functions himself.

But shortly after the United States entered World War II, the Office of War Information (OWI) was established and was placed under the direction of radio newsman Elmer Davis. The State Department assumed control of other information functions.

Information officers—primarily ex-journalists, advertising and public relations men—worked under the authority of the ambassadors. In addition to their duties of disseminating propaganda abroad, they also employed domestic "propaganda" programs to promote war bonds and secrecy, using such slogans as "Keep it Under Your Stetson."[20]

Shortly after the end of WWII, Truman dissolved the Office of

War Information and moved most of the international information functions to the State Department. Truman appointed advertising executive William Benton of Benton & Bowles Advertising Agency as the first head of the information agency with the rank of Assistant Secretary of State for Public Affairs. The title was similar to the one held almost 60 years later by ad executive Charlotte Beers.

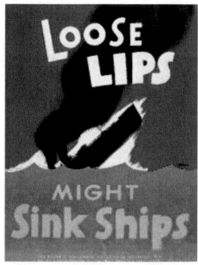

A World War II propaganda poster promoting secrecy

The agency was expanded in 1946 with the passage of the Fulbright Act, which funded international academic exchanges and eventually became the Office of International Information and Education Exchange in 1947.

In 1948, Congress gave official statutory authority for a government information agency outside of wartime by passing the Smith-Mundt Act. The objectives of the act were "to promote a mutual understanding between the people of the United States and the people of other countries."[21] The act forbade the American government from propagandizing its own people and housed the information agency within the State Department, where it functioned under the subordination of the foreign service officers.

During the Korean War, the International Information Agency (IIA) was operating at a peak budget of $96 million and about 13,500 employees.[22] It was dramatically downsized in 1953 due to political turmoil resulting from accusations of Sen. Joseph McCarthy that the IIA had ties to communism. Budgets and personnel were immediately cut.

The agency's struggle ended in August 1953 when the United

States Information Agency (USIA) was created, independent of the State Department.[23] The change reduced the conflicts between communications personnel and the diplomatic corps, as the information function was housed in a separate bureaucracy, but its programs remained in coordination and under the oversight of the foreign service officers.

In the years that followed, Soviet expansion became a clear threat to the United States, and although no official "Cold War" was declared, an ideological battle waged between the United States and the Soviet Union for almost 50 years. As the Cold War heated up, so did the American propaganda machine.

In order to combat the misinformation and deceptive stories coming from the Soviet Union about the horrors of capitalism, America responded with similar charges about communism. According to Leo Bogart's study of the USIA, 160 U.S. Information Service libraries operated throughout the world in 1953 and 1954. A daily press service was distributed to 10,000 newspapers. Twenty-five periodicals were published, from comic books to high-level textbooks on communism. More than 400 reels of film footage were produced, and movies in 22 different languages were shown worldwide.[24]

Voice of America

One of the most effective Cold War weapons of public diplomacy (or propaganda) was the Voice of America (VOA).

VOA first began broadcasting in February 24, 1942, to German-occupied Europe and North Africa. VOA programs originally transmitted information about America's war objectives and post-war plans. Originally established under the Office of War Information, VOA was moved to the State Department after WWII and continued to operate during the Cold War as the voice of anti-communism around the world.[25]

VOA was considered the "heart" of USIA operations during the

Cold War. Broadcasts into the Soviet Union began as early as February 1947 and continue today primarily through VOA "sister" stations Radio Free Europe and Radio Liberty.

Some consider VOA one of the most important tools in public diplomacy and credit it for playing an influential role in America's winning the Cold War. People in the far-flung regions of the Soviet Union recall hearing about the uprisings in Moscow and the subsequent fall of the communist government over the Voice of America.

This encouraged similar movements throughout the Soviet Union and probably played a significant role in the break-up of the USSR in 1991. Numerous anecdotal stories about the VOA's influence on regular people living in politically oppressed countries during the Cold War are told and re-told.

In his book *American Propaganda Abroad,* Fitzhugh Green, a Foreign Information Officer and 16-year employee of USIA, relays one such story that took place on a crowded street in Beijing during the early 1980s. A Chinese student who, when questioned in fluent Mandarin by an American wire service reporter about why he was so patient rather than pushing to see the latest wall newspaper like the others on the street, responded, "No hurry, I've already heard the news on the Voice of America."[26]

The Voice of America patterns itself after the BBC in its attempt to present informative and objective news coverage, but as the official broadcasting service of the U.S. government, everything it presents must be consistent with U.S. policy. VOA might be considered white propaganda as it delivers informational and analytical programming about America to audiences abroad.

The balance between governmental influence and journalistic standards of objective reporting is a matter of constant debate. Over the years, VOA has attempted to remain independent. The recent placement of VOA under the Broadcasting Board of Governors (BBG), a group of eight independent members from industry and the

Secretary of State, was an attempt at continued autonomy. However, disagreements about the style and approach of the broadcasts persist.

Currently, the Voice of America reaches millions of listeners around the world each week with news, news analysis and cultural programming about American life. According to the VOA Web site (www.voanews.com), the station broadcasts 1,000 hours of programming each week in 44 languages from Afan Oromo to Vietnamese.

Domestic and overseas reporters file 150 news reports a day. In addition to its 24-hour-a-day radio transmission, VOA is also streamed over the World Wide Web, which allows American audiences to hear its programming. This is something that, until recently, was impossible because of the Congressional prohibition against government media outlets aimed directly at Americans (except via short-wave radio). As noted earlier, most Americans have never heard the Voice of America, but it is one of the most recognized stations in international broadcasting.

In fiscal year 2004, Congress appropriated $151 million to support VOA and its 1,190 employees, who are stationed at home and overseas. VOA continues to be an important and influential source of news and information for audiences across the globe.

Edward R. Murrow

At the height of the Cold War, Edward R. Murrow, joined the government to serve as chief communications consultant to President John F. Kennedy.

With Murrow at the helm of the USIA from 1961 to 1964, the agency gained some clout, but it still did not have consistent access to the President as Murrow wished. This shortcoming became apparent during the Bay of Pigs invasion.

After the crisis, Murrow was put in charge of explaining U.S. actions to the foreign media—not an easy task when most of the decision making happened without his knowledge. Murrow was later

quoted as saying to President
Kennedy, "Mr. President, I
have to [be included in] the
take-offs as well as the crash
landings in order to be able to
inform you and advise you on
how the message is going to
play, how the message should
be crafted."[27]

Edward R. Murrow on Voice of
America radio (Photo courtesy
of the Voice of America)

The USIA reached its
zenith under Edward R.
Murrow but continued to
function throughout the 1970s and 80s until the end of the Cold War,
when the importance of propaganda and public diplomacy faded.
Under the Clinton Administration, public diplomacy budgets were
dramatically slashed.[28]

In 1999, with pressure from Congress, the USIA was absorbed
back into the State Department.

U.S. Public Diplomacy Functions and Agencies

After WWI, America's information agency underwent many
changes in leadership, name and organization. Broadly speaking, CPI
became the forerunner of the USIA, which served as the central
public diplomacy/propaganda agency for the U.S. government for
most of the 20th century. USIA maintained its independence during
the Cold War, before being folded back into the State Department,
where it is housed today.

In his book *American Propaganda Abroad,* Fitzhugh Green
provides a detailed history of the U.S. government's information
agency from the Creel Committee during WWI through the period of
the USIA and the Cold War. Green notes how the government's
propaganda arm has been moved around in the bureaucratic maze and
re-named multiple times. He compares the American government's

treatment of its information agency to the way "homemakers handle living room furniture—no arrangement suits for very long."[29]

The Foreign Affairs Reform and Restructuring Act passed by Congress in 1998 placed the USIA back into the State Department. The first Under Secretary of Public Diplomacy and Public Affairs, Evelyn Lieberman, said the goal would be to marry public diplomacy and traditional diplomacy successfully, because in an age of global communications "diplomacy wears an increasingly public face."[30]

On October 1, 1999, USIA shut its doors and the State Department assumed responsibility for most overseas information programs. The international exchange programs (including Fulbright) were moved to a newly created Bureau of Educational and Cultural Affairs within the State Department. Authority over government-sponsored broadcasting services, including the Voice of America, was placed with the Broadcasting Board of Governors.

Propaganda Research

Social scientists, mass communication practitioners and politicians have long been interested in understanding the power of propaganda and the process through which carefully crafted messages can move the so-called masses toward uniform thought and action. The academic interest in propaganda was at its height following World War I—a time when political movements like fascism and communism were sweeping Europe largely through the effective use of propaganda.

American politicians, scientists and thinkers of the day grew concerned about the likelihood that subversive political groups could use powerful propaganda techniques to infiltrate and indoctrinate Americans against capitalism and democracy. Elites feared that any attempt at using propaganda on a naive American population would prove immediate and effective, thus "ruining" the American way of life as they knew it.

The fear of propaganda was fueled by two major psychological theories popular in the 1930s. One was behaviorism, which revolved around the belief that all human action is conditioned responses to external environmental stimuli. The other was Freudianism, which held that the pleasure-seeking id could override the rational ego.

These theories contributed to the idea that mass media could have have powerful effects on the masses in a direct, uniform and instantaneous manner—or what later came to be known as the Magic Bullet or Hypodermic Needle theory.

These theories convinced many of the intellectual elites of the day—including Walter Lippmann, Harold Lasswell and John Dewey—that subversive propaganda, if used on the American people, could have devastating, instant and powerful effects, which could even destroy the American way of life.

As a result, Lippmann and Lasswell, among others, called for the scientific technocracy (the academic elite of the time) to maintain strict control of the media. Lippmann was a pessimist when it came to democratic theory. He believed that an educated elite of political scientists should guide public policy.

In contrast, Dewey, a defender of democracy and public education, believed the media could be used to educate the masses and "interest the public in public interests."[31] He had faith that average Americans could protect themselves from the lies of propaganda, if properly educated. Dewey's work later influenced the movement to teach public school children about the devices of propaganda as a way to protect themselves from its ill effects.

The prevailing wisdom was that propaganda had strong effects on people—that the average American was generally vulnerable. Out of this environment, the Institute for Propaganda Analysis was established in 1937. A wealthy merchant named Edward Filene funded the Institute and asked Princeton professor Hadley Cantril to be its first president. The Institute's goals were to understand the processes and effects of propaganda and, ultimately, to teach Americans how to protect themselves from it.[32]

War of the Worlds

One of Cantril's first major research projects also seemed to reinforce the idea that propaganda could have powerful effects.

On October 30, 1938, CBS radio's Mercury Theater presented a special Halloween audio dramatic presentation of H.G. Wells' book *War of the Worlds.* Radio personality Orson Welles was the brains behind the project, as well as one of the on-air narrators. Several disclaimers were broadcast before and during the presentation, but many people didn't hear them and they panicked, believing Martians had actually landed on Earth.

Orson Welles performing for CBS radio (Photo courtesy of the *Toronto Star*)

The drama used realistic audio techniques such as news bulletins, interruptions of the "regularly scheduled music programming" and "on-the-scene reporters" to disguise the fiction. CBS apologized and Welles said he never intended to deceive the public into thinking the Martian landing was real.

Working at Princeton in the Office of Radio Research, Hadley Cantril immediately saw an opportunity to learn about the power of propaganda from the *War of the Worlds* incident and launched a research study of the program's effects within a short time after its broadcast.

Cantril and his team of researchers addressed three research questions: What was the extent of the panic? Why did this broadcast frighten some people when other fantastic broadcasts did not? And why did this broadcast frighten some people, but not others?

Cantril and his team conducted personal interviews and surveyed listeners.[33] They analyzed newspaper reports and letters to CBS about the public's reaction to the broadcast. They found that 28 percent of the 6 million

Professor Hadley Cantril (Photo courtesy of the Princeton University Library)

people who listened to the broadcast believed Martians were actually landing on earth. Of those, about 70 percent of those actually panicked (estimated to be 1.2 million).

The program's believability was attributed to its sheer dramatic excellence; the fact that the radio was the predominant source of news, particularly breaking news; and the use of real places and expert sources such as scientists at Princeton University. The historical timing of the broadcast also played a role. The world was an unstable place in 1938. Deep in an economic depression with war raging in Europe, Americans were feeling uneasy—many said that they could readily believe that the world was coming to an end.

Another important element to the vast and rapid acceptance of the message was the fact that many listeners tuned in late. The more popular competing radio show featured comparatively uninteresting guests that evening, so many listeners switched stations at about five minutes into the program. This was just late enough to miss the Mercury Radio Theater initial disclaimer stating that the show was a science-fiction drama and not a real news story.

Perhaps the most important contribution of Cantril's research to the understanding of propaganda was his explanation of why some audience members were frightened while others were not. Cantril and his co-researchers found that personality factors played a role. Listeners with phobic personalities, lack of self-confidence and emotional insecurity were more likely to believe that Martians had landed.

Less educated and more religious listeners also were more likely to believe the broadcast. The role of opinion leaders also was present in Cantril's study, though he did not label it as such. Listeners who were told by a friend to tune in because Martians had landed in New Jersey were more likely to believe than those who tuned in on their own.[34]

Cantril's findings appeared to confirm elites' worst fears. Americans could be susceptible to false mass media messages and could easily be convinced that something was true if they heard it on the airwaves. Propaganda was effective and needed to be controlled.

Paradoxically, though, Cantril's study also ushered in the age of "limited effects." Although many people panicked after hearing the *War of the Worlds* broadcast, his study showed that the effects were not uniform. People who had phobic personalities and less education and those who were more religious were more likely to panic. But it would be another decade or so before the so-called "limited effects model" would dominate research on the effects of mass media. One early study contributing to this new "paradigm" was the "Why We Fight" Films.

"Why We Fight" Films

The bombing of Pearl Harbor thrust the United States into another World War. The attention of media researchers turned to how the U.S. government could use mass media to convince young men to enlist in the military and to motivate them to fight the Germans.

Troop morale was a significant problem for the U.S. military as America entered WWII. A Kansas newspaper reporter at the time characterized the troops as not having "the slightest enthusiasm for this war or this cause. They are not grouchy, they are not mutinous, they just don't give a tinker's dam."[35]

America's pre-war isolationism and rapid entry into the war left the military with young men who knew little about overseas affairs or U.S. foreign policy and had little interest in fighting in Europe. Turning citizens into soldiers was an important and immediate task for the military.

Recognizing the attitude problem, Army Chief of Staff General George Marshall leveraged the talents of popular Hollywood film director Frank Capra in 1942 for the Morale Branch. Marshall asked Capra to create "a series of documentary, factual information films that will explain to our boys why we are fighting and the principles for which we are fighting" (Capra quoting Marshall).[36]

The resulting work produced a series of seven films known as the *Why We Fight* films, which were shown to recruits during their training. The films were 50-minute documentaries that were objective and factual in tone, covering topics from the rise of fascism in Europe to America's entry into the war after Pearl Harbor.

The War Department's goals were to transfer factual knowledge and shape attitudes about the war in such a way that the young soldiers would be ready and willing to fight. The content of each of the films addressed these goals, but the War Department needed to know—were the films working as hoped?

To answer this question, they turned to a group of distinguished scientists, including Yale psychologist Carl I. Hovland. Hovland's team used experimental research to measure the ability of the films to transfer knowledge and shape attitudes and opinions among military recruits. Working with the Army, the scientists were given control over when, where and who would see the films. The Army provided background data on the recruits and gave the scientists complete access and funding to conduct their studies.

Multiple experiments were administered using combinations of films and variations of test and control groups, measurement instruments and pre/post conditions. One film, *The Battle of Britain*, was tested individually, as it contained an abundance of factual information about the war and emphasized confidence in the Allies.

A pre/post control group test of this film found that factual information was acquired about Germany's bombing of Great Britain, the British resistance and the outstanding performance of the Royal Air Force. Opinions about and interpretations of these military events were somewhat changed after viewing the film. However, the film had little effect on general attitudes toward the British allies and showed no effect toward the ultimate goal of motivating the soldiers to fight.[37] These findings, along with other mass communication research of the time, altered the prevailing paradigm about the effects of mass communication. Scientists began to doubt the media's power to shape the masses.

After WWII, researchers continued to study media effects, and they discovered that differences among audience members, source factors and message design impacted effectiveness to varying degrees. Hovland continued after the war to work on the experimental study of attitude change. His experience with the Army films eventually led to the early principles of persuasion theory, which are discussed briefly in Chapter 5.

Propaganda Devices

As president of the Institute for Propaganda Analysis, Hadley Cantril focused the organization's efforts on educating Americans, particularly school children, on the methods of propaganda so that they might be inoculated against anti-American messages.

Over its brief history from 1937 to 1942, the Institute for

Propaganda Analysis published several books. One of the most famous was *The Fine Art of Propaganda* by Alfred McClung Lee and Elizabeth Briant Lee.[38]

The Lee and Lee book used clever names to identify seven propaganda devices that could be easily taught in the public schools. They were glittering generality, transfer, testimonial, plain folks, card stacking, bandwagon and name-calling.

These seven devices are fairly simplistic and do not take into consideration other elements of persuasive communication, such as credibility of the sender and differences among audience members. However, the seven devices provide a practical method for examining propaganda programs and can be used to analyze the Shared Values Initiative.

A Propaganda Analysis of the Shared Values Initiative

To answer the question posed in the title of this chapter, it is helpful to examine Lee and Lee's propaganda devices as they are used in the five SVI television spots. There is no evidence to suggest, however, that these devices were purposefully employed in developing the SVI campaign.

Glittering Generality

Lee and Lee defined "glittering generality" as "associating something with a 'virtue word' to encourage blind approval."[39]

One could argue that use of the "Shared Values" label for the propaganda initiative is itself an example of a glittering generality, because it focuses on the positive only and not the vast cultural and political differences between non-Muslim and Muslim Americans.

Transfer

According to Lee and Lee, "transfer carries the authority, sanction, and prestige of something respected and revered over to something else in order to make the latter more acceptable." Transfer operates by way of associating something positive with an idea or message in the hopes that the positive elements will "rub off" on the message.

The use of icons and symbols was evident in the SVI spots. Iconic images of the American family and baseball were used alongside pictures of Muslim women with their heads covered, Muslims kneeling and praying in public places, the Hasidic Jewish pedestrian on the Manhattan sidewalk and a female public school teacher holding religious classes for children in her home on Saturdays.

In addition, the final frames of SVI commercials could also qualify for the "transfer" label because they associated sponsorship of the advertisements with a nonprofit Muslim organization (CAMU) that appears to have been created for the specific purpose of dissociating the messages from the State Department.

Testimonial

Testimonials involve "having some respected or hated person say that a given idea or program or product or person is good or bad."[40]

The format of the SVI spots contains testimonials from Muslims living in the United States: a doctor, a baker, a journalism student, a school teacher and a paramedic firefighter. According to Beers, using American Muslims as spokespersons instead of non-Muslim Americans was considered a much more effective approach.

Plain Folks

An attempt to convince audience members that a speaker's ideas are good because they are "of the people" is known as plain folks.[41]

The use of American Muslims who represent "regular people next door" going about their business and family lives is clearly an example of the plain folks approach. The characters in the commercials are shown at work, at home, at school, during prayer, at a carnival and sporting events, and in many cases they are interacting with their plain folk non-Muslim counterparts.

The use of plain folks is in keeping with Beers' strategy of crafting a campaign "from the people and to the people."

Card Stacking

Card stacking involves "selection and use of facts or falsehoods, illustrations or distractions, and logical or illogical statements in order to give the best or worst possible case for an idea, program, person or product."[42]

Card stacking is apparent with the use of selected evidence to make the point that Muslims are treated well in America today while ignoring well-documented evidence that there was, indeed, mistreatment of some Muslims in the United States after 9/11.

Bandwagon

The message "everybody—at least all of us—is doing it" is the bandwagon technique.[43] Bandwagon invokes a group of people to which the target might belong or aspire to belong.

A message directed to Muslims by Muslim spokespersons unanimous in their statements that they are leading happy lives in the United States is a clear example of bandwagon technique. There is no suggestion from any of the speakers that any of their Muslim acquaintances experienced anything less than acceptance in America.

Beyond the on-camera speakers was the sponsorship of the campaign by the Council of American Muslims for Understanding (CAMU), as evidenced by the superimposed tagline, which was followed by the line "and the American people." These third-party endorsers of the campaign presumably were used in an effort to add credibility to the message.

Name-calling

"Giving an idea a bad label ... to make us reject and condemn the idea without examining the evidence"[44] was notably absent from SVI, although it is a common technique in much propaganda, especially during wartime.

After 9/11, President George W. Bush and other officials made much use of the "terrorist" label in condemning acts of violence. However, the SVI spots steered clear of any negative language and the word "terrorism" was never mentioned.

Conclusion

The SVI advertisements clearly contained many of the elements that Lee and Lee defined as being associated with propaganda. And many critics argue that SVI was propaganda. But is that label justified? Or should SVI be called public diplomacy or simply persuasive communication?

Although each reader will have to make his or her own determination about the content of SVI, we believe the SVI spots were generally truthful, and the main message—that Americans are generally tolerant of Muslims and other religious groups—was accurately portrayed. The SVI spots were very much like commercial advertising, which almost always emphasizes and sometimes exaggerates the positive aspects of a product or service and almost always ignores the negative aspects.

Although reasonable people may disagree about whether the SVI spots deserve the label propaganda, SVI clearly was a new approach to public diplomacy—one that used advertising to fight the war on terrorism. The State Department also employed other new approaches to public diplomacy after 9/11. These are explored in the next chapter.

Chapter Endnotes

[1]Werner J. Severin and James W. Tankard, *Communication Theories, Origins, Methods and Uses in Mass Media,* 5th ed. (New York: Longman, 2001), p. 110.
[2]Ibid.
[3]Harold D. Lasswell, *Propaganda Technique in the World War* (New York: Peter Smith, 1927).
[4]Harold D. Lasswell, "Propaganda," in E. R. A. Seligman and A. Johnson, eds., *Encyclopedia of the Social Sciences, Vol. 12* (New York: McMillian, 1937), pp. 521-528.
[5]Stanley J. Baran and Dennis K. Davis, *Mass Communication Theory: Foundations, Ferment and Future,* 3rd ed. (Belmont, CA: Wadsworth, 2003).
[6]William Powers, "Brand of the free*" National Journal,33,* 17 November 2001, p. 357.
[7]Garth Jowett, and Victoria O'Donnell, *Propaganda and Persuasion,* 3rd ed. (Thousand Oaks, CA: Sage Publications, 1999).
[8]This approach doesn't mean that a message that contains truth-statements can never be classified as propaganda. If the truth-statement leads to misinterpretations, then it can still be considered as misleading or as distortion. It also doesn't mean that organizations that deliberately create misinformation may also from time to time produce nonpropagandistic messages. Instead, the label "propaganda" technically can be applied only after analyzing a message as well as its impact or effects on audiences.
[9]Garth Jowett, "Toward a propaganda analysis of the Gulf War," in *Desert Storm and the Mass Media,* Bradley Greenberg and Walter Gantz, eds. (New Jersey: Hampton Press, 1993), p. 75.
[10]Richard Nelson, *A Chronology and Glossary of Propaganda in the United States* (Westport, CT and London: Greenwood Press. 1996).
[11]"Diplomacy." *Encyclopædia Britannica,* 2005. Encyclopædia Britannica Premium Service. 27 Oct. 2005 <http://www.britannica.com/eb/article-9106182>.
[12]Gregg Wolper, "Wilsonian public diplomacy: The Committee on Public Information in Spain," *Diplomatic History,* 17 (1993): p. 17.
[13]Leo Bogart, *Cool Words, Cold War: A New Look at USIA's premises for Propaganda,* revised ed. (Washington D.C.:American University Press, 1995).
[14]Nancy Snow, *Propaganda, Inc.: Selling America's Culture to the World.* 2nd ed. (New York: Seven Stories Press, 2002).

[15]Wolper, "Wilsonian public diplomacy," p. 17.

[16]Wolper, "Wilsonian public diplomacy," p. 19.

[17]As retold in Snow and in Fitzhugh Green, *American Propaganda Abroad* (New York: Hippocrene Books, 1988).

[18]See Snow and Green.

[19]George Creel, *How We Advertised America: The First Telling of the Amazing Story of the Committee on Public Information that Carried the Gospel of Americanism to Every Corner of the Globe.* (New York: Harper & Brothers, 1920).

[20]Powers, "Brand of the Free," p. 357-9.

[21]Bogart, *Cool Words*.

[22]Ibid.

[23]Green, *American Propaganda*, p. 25.

[24]Bogart, *Cool Words*, p. xiv.

[25]David F. Krugler, *The Voice of America and the Domestic Propaganda Battles, 1945-1953* (Columbia, MO: University of Missouri Press, 2000).

[26]Green, *American Propaganda*, p. 78.

[27]Green, *American Propaganda*, p. 36.

[28]Anne Kornblut, "Problems of image, diplomacy beset United States, *Boston Globe* 9 March 2003, p. A25.

[29]Green, *American Propaganda* p. 32.

[30]Evelyn Lieberman, "Diplomacy redefined: Closing the public information gap," *Washington Times*, 5 October 1999.

[31]See Baran and Davis, *Mass Communication Theory* for a full discussion of early Propaganda Theory.

[32]Severin and Tankard, *Communication Theories,* p. 110.

[33]As reported in Shearon Lowery, and Melvin DeFleur, *Milestones in Mass Communication Research: Media Effects*, 3rd ed. (White Plains, NY: Longman, 1995).

[34]Ibid. p. 63.

[35]William Allen White to White House adviser Lowell Mellett (Sept. 1940), retrieved from http://history.acusd.edu.gen/filmnotes/whywefight.html on Feb. 3, 2006.

[36]Frank Capra, *The Name Above the Title: An Autobiography* (New York: Macmillan, 1971), p. 327.

[37]As reported in Lowery and DeFleur, *Milestones in Mass Communication Research*.

[38]Alfred Lee & Elizabeth Briant Lee, *The Fine Art of Propaganda: A study of Father Coughlin's speeches* (New York: Harcourt, Brace & Company, 1939).

[39]Ibid, p. 47.

[40]Ibid, p. 74.

[41]Ibid, p. 92.

[42]Ibid, p. 95.
[43]Ibid, p. 105.
[44]Ibid, p. 26.

Chapter 3

New Approaches to Public Diplomacy

Since 9/11, the U.S. government has employed many other forms of public diplomacy beyond the Shared Values Initiative. This chapter focuses on those programs, which included a magazine for Arab teens, brochures about the horrors of Saddam Hussein and an advertising campaign to encourage Americans to provide tips leading to the arrest of terrorists. This chapter also explores and evaluates the nonbroadcast components of the Shared Values Initiative, which included print and radio ads and programs.

The Shared Values Initiative (SVI) commercials, as described in Chapter 1 (see Table 1.2 and Appendix A), represented only one of the new approaches to public diplomacy implemented after 9/11.

When Charlotte Beers first took office in October 2001, she immediately began applying her consumer marketing approach to the job of telling America's story in the Arab and Muslim world. Prior to launching SVI in late 2002, Beers developed numerous other public diplomacy programs that were new to the State Department.

They included placement of U.S. spokespeople on popular international media, distribution of four-color magazines and posters featuring Muslim life in America, and revamping the State Department's Rewards for Justice programs.

Public Relations in Public Diplomacy

The placement of a spokesperson in the popular media is a public relations tactic often used by consumer marketers, politicians and advocacy groups.

Almost immediately after her appointment, Beers adopted this tactic at the State Department. She enlisted Christopher Ross, a former ambassador to Syria who was fluent in Arabic, as a spokesman on Middle Eastern television news programs to present America's side of the story after 9/11. Ambassador Ross had been "underused," according to Beers, who saw the need to have a fluent Arabic speaker representing the United States on Arabic television, including Al-Jazeera.

Other government officials, including National Security Adviser Condoleezza Rice and Secretary of Defense Donald Rumsfeld, gave interviews on Al-Jazeera and other Middle Eastern broadcast stations. When they spoke, station personnel translated their English into the local language. In the case of Christopher Ross, audiences heard the words of a top U.S. government official in their own language—a very powerful communication tool.

Secretary Powell on MTV

In another bold move, Beers helped engineer a broadcast of Secretary of State Colin Powell interacting with young people around the world on MTV's "Be Heard."[1]

During the program, Powell fielded questions via a satellite link from a live global audience of about 200 young people in Sao Paulo, Milan, Cairo, Moscow, New Delhi and London. Seventy-five American twenty-somethings also asked questions in the Washington, D.C., studio that hosted Powell.

The program was taped on Valentine's Day morning 2002 and was broadcast that evening across the United States. It aired later that

month internationally. MTV
projected that the show
reached 370 million people in
164 countries.[2]

Powell was very
comfortable with the young
people's questions, including
one from a Norwegian woman
who asked, "How do you feel
about representing a country
commonly perceived as the
Satan of contemporary
politics?"

Secretary of State Colin Powell
appears on MTV

Powell responded, "Seen as what?"

The young woman repeated herself: "As the Satan of
contemporary politics."

Powell replied, "Satan, Oh."

After the audience laughed, Powell said quickly and
confidently, "Well, I reject the characterization." He then explained
how throughout modern history America had gone to war to protect
people around the world and defend their freedoms and took nothing
in return. "The only land we ever asked for was enough land to bury
our dead."

Reviews of the broadcast were generally positive, noting
Powell's ease in communicating with a younger generation about
serious global issues, including Kashmir, the Taliban and the Israeli-
Palestinian conflict.

However, the comment that garnered the most press coverage
had less to do with international politics than with the domestic battle
between conservatives and liberals in the United States. When an
Italian girl asked about the Roman Catholic Church's ban on
condoms, Powell delicately replied that he supported the use of
condoms as a way to protect against disease. Some observers
concluded that Powell was not in agreement with President Bush on

the issue of abstinence and was not on the same page with the President on other issues.

White House Press Secretary Ari Fleischer denied that speculation, reminding the press that Secretary Powell had the full support of the President. The incident, although small news at the time, may have been a foreshadowing of larger problems leading to Powell's resignation as Secretary of State.

Powell's appearance was billed as a "global discussion" by the producers of MTV, who welcomed the idea as a chance to position the cable network as an outlet for political discourse as well as for music videos. This wasn't the first time a top official had appeared on MTV. President Bill Clinton appeared in 1994 and, among more serious topics, announced his preference for boxers over briefs.

But Powell's appearance was an opportunity for the State Department to "rebrand" America, according to some observers. And it was, no doubt, a strategy consistent with Beers' communication objectives while at the State Department.

Beers incorporated a small video clip of Secretary Powell on MTV into her public presentations later that year. She encouraged U.S. ambassadors around the world to do the same.

Beers used Powell's television appearance was an example of the positive impact that mass media, an effective spokesman and a simple message can have on influencing global attitudes toward America. She praised Powell's smooth communication style and emphasized the power and influence he could have on international audiences around the world.

Hi Magazine

In another attempt to promote dialogue with young audiences in the Middle East and engender them to American cultural values, Beers proposed a magazine aimed at Arab teens.

Her idea eventually led to the launching of *Hi* magazine, but it didn't appear until after her resignation. The name *Hi* was chosen because it is a word commonly used by Arab young people, as with American young people, as a casual greeting.

Hi's first issue in July 2003 hit newsstands in several countries—Algeria, Bahrain, Cyprus, Egypt, Greece, Israel, Jordan, Kuwait, Lebanon, Morocco, Syria, the Gaza Strip, Tunisia, Sudan, Saudi Arabia, Qatar, Oman, Yemen, the United Arab Emirates and the West Bank. The price was about $2, less than most Arab

The cover of an issue of *Hi* magazine.

magazines. It was a slick, colorful publication targeted to young Arabs between the ages of 18 and 35.

Although funded by the State Department, the magazine didn't contain a lot of political content. Its goal, according to State Department officials, was to give the younger generation in the Middle East a window on American life and make them aware of American values.

The first issues featured stories about Arab-American college students and Arab-American actor Tony Shalhoub along with a discussion about the debate over smoking in America.[3] *Hi* magazine featured news and articles that were interesting to young people around the world, such as music, entertainment, technology, fashion and health.

The Washington Post and other critics questioned why discussions of Middle East policy,[4] al Qaeda and the Palestinian situation were absent from the pages of *Hi*. Creators responded that the magazine was aimed to "fill a niche between political news publications and glossy beauty and fashion by offering cultural information about the United States not readily available in the Middle East."[5]

The magazine cost American taxpayers $4.2 million annually. A third party contractor, the Washington-based Magazine Group, was responsible for the creation and production of the magazine. Articles were written by American and Arab journalists and submitted to the State Department for final approval.

The magazine carried some advertising. Cadbury Chocolates was featured in the first issue. But advertising only brought in a small amount of revenue.

State Department officials hoped the magazine would become popular enough to be self-supporting.[6] The State Department claimed circulation was 50,000, but some observers questioned these figures. One Egyptian vendor reported ordering 50 copies but only selling 10. In December 2005, while this book was in production, new Under Secretary of State Karen Hughes suspended publication of *Hi* magazine pending a review of its readership and effectiveness.

The Arab language Internet edition of *Hi* (www.himag.com) encourages interactive dialogue and urges readers to provide feedback to editors. One feature called "Ask America" invites readers to submit questions about America, American life and culture.

About one year after the magazine first appeared, a Web site called Hi International (www.hiinternational.com) was launched in English to reach international audiences beyond the Arab world with similar content. Both sites are still operating.

Rewards for Justice

Another project Beers took on when she came to the State Department was reviving a long-used communication program called "Rewards for Justice."

Rewards for Justice provides monetary rewards for information leading to the arrest of known terrorists. In the style of Wild West wanted posters, the State Department's Diplomatic Security division circulates information about wanted terrorists through a Web site (www.rewardsforjustice.net). Posters, leaflets and even matchbook covers are also distributed overseas.

According to the State Department, the program, which began in 1984, has paid out almost $10 million since 1997. A total of $25 million is available for information leading to the arrest or capture of Osama bin Laden.

When Beers came to the State Department, the Rewards for Justice program officers eagerly invited her to use her advertising expertise to help improve their materials. Beers was happy to do so, and called on her former agency, Ogilvy and Mather, to produce the new creative materials. Prior to their involvement, Rewards for Justice ads looked like wanted posters, featuring large mug shots of scruffy terrorists along with their biographical data and information about how to call in tips and collect rewards.

Beers suggested a different approach. First she recommended expanding the program to Americans as well as international citizens, saying, "before September 11th it might have been unthinkable for us to say, 'among us lives a terrorist.' And now it is unquestioned."[7]

Beers also sought research data about the appropriate target audience for the campaign. She asked counter-terrorism experts who they believed to be the most likely in a community to have information about terrorists and who would be most willing to turn them in. After some discussion, the experts agreed that women—mothers, wives, sisters—were often in possession of the most reliable information about terrorists and were also the most likely to want to stop them.

Using this information, Beers recommended that the grizzly and gory Rewards for Justice posters be replaced with more subtle ads that appealed to women and their desire to keep their families and communities safe. One ad featured the headline, *Can a Woman Stop*

=== *A Way to Protect Your Family and Others in Your Community* ===

CAN A WOMAN
STOP TERRORISM?

You, as a woman and perhaps a mother, may be in a unique position to act against international terrorism. You know what is happening within your family, your neighborhood, your town or village. You are part of a worldwide network of awareness. What you may know or see may bear witness to a plan to commit an act of unspeakable violence.

The U.S. Government has a program called Rewards for Justice whereby you can communicate what you know in strict confidence.

You may be eligible for a reward, which you can use to build a future for your family and start a new life. This may also give you an opportunity to pay for a home and educate your children. In addition to a cash reward, personal protection is available, which may include moving you and your family to a safe location.

For anyone, such a telephone call would be an act of extraordinary bravery. For you, as a woman, it is also a way to enable a child, a true innocent, to live to choose a path, to worship God, to return the love of a mother.

If you have information that could prevent an international terrorist act, or could bring to justice persons who have committed one, today is the day to speak out. There is no cultural standard, no holy law or writ, no custom of silence on the face of the earth that permits children to die.

There is a telephone in your home. A pay phone on a corner where you live or work. A cell phone lying somewhere nearby. A pen with which you can write a letter.

Will you pick it up, and stop a terrorist?

> **Do you have information that could prevent a terrorist act?**
>
> •
>
> Contact: *Your local police, the FBI, or the nearest U.S. Embassy or Consulate.*
>
> •
>
> Call: *1-800-USREWARDS*
>
> •
>
> E-mail: *mail@rewardsforjustice.net*

REWARDS UP TO $25 MILLION

CONTACT: Your local police, the FBI, or the nearest U.S. Embassy or Consulate. CALL: 1-800-USREWARDS. E-MAIL: mail@rewardsforjustice.net. *Rewards of up to $25 million, protection of your identity, and relocation of your family may be available for persons providing information that prevents an international terrorist act against U.S. persons or property or brings to justice persons who have committed one. To date, more than $8 million has been paid.*

Your call or e-mail will be kept strictly confidential.

REWARDS FOR JUSTICE

1.800.USREWARDS
www.rewardsforjustice.net

U.S. Department of State

Terrorism?

"[M]y personal bias is that women are very observant and thoughtful about these things," Beers said about the ad.[8] "In this approach, we're talking about protecting your family and your community. The consequences of a terrorist act is obviously devastating to a family and community, as we now know all too well."

The updated and overhauled Rewards for Justice advertising campaign was presented to the public during a State Department press briefing on December 13, 2001. Secretary of State Powell began the briefing and announced the new program, saying, "Today, for the first time, we are rolling out an extensive domestic media campaign to support the Rewards for Justice Program. This program will distribute public service announcements to every major media market in the United States."[9] He introduced Beers and Assistant Secretary David Carpenter from Diplomatic Security as the two people most responsible for the new campaign.

Beers said the program marked the first time the Rewards for Justice program had been made available to U.S. citizens. She explained that it would be translated into 30 languages and launched internationally in January 2002.

Beers asked mass media companies to run the ads free of charge on their stations and in their newspapers. She announced that *The Washington Post* was running one of the ads that day and that other newspapers across the country were doing the same. She also announced commitments from ABC radio and from a program director at KONE-FM in Lubbock, Texas. Journalists at the conference received a computer disc containing copies of the print and radio ads.

During the Rewards for Justice press conference Beers also introduced two Connecticut businessmen, Scott Case and Joe Rutledge, who launched a Rewards for Justice fund drive in tandem with the rollout of the State Department's campaign. Case and Rutledge, who had backgrounds in Web-based marketing, assisted Beers in re-designing the Rewards for Justice Web site. Additionally they created a Web site and a toll-free telephone line to provide a way for individual Americans to donate funds to the Rewards for

---

The Price of Freedom

DO REWARDS WORK AGAINST TERRORISM?

They do. In more than twenty cases, the Rewards for Justice program has paid more than 8 million dollars for information that prevented international terrorist acts or helped bring to justice those involved in prior acts.

Consider these examples. They are based on classified information, and details have been fictionalized to protect identities. But they are real-life instances where rewards were paid:

1. After the 1993 bombing of the World Trade Center in New York, accused bomber Ramzi Ahmed Yousef fled the U.S. Leaflets and posters, even matchbooks, were distributed worldwide seeking this fugitive. Not long after, an informant offered a tip regarding Yousef's whereabouts. He was captured in Pakistan and is now in jail in the U.S. The informant received a reward for sharing this knowledge.

2. Forty-eight hours before an airport bombing was set to occur, it was stopped by a brave young man who stepped forward with information. The terrorists had already assembled automatic weapons, grenades, and explosives. The young man received a significant reward, and his family was relocated to a safe place. Hundreds of lives were saved.

> Do you have information that could prevent a terrorist act?
>
> Contact: *Your local police, the FBI, or the nearest U.S. Embassy or Consulate.*
>
> •
>
> Call: *1-800-USREWARDS*
>
> •
>
> E-mail: *mail@rewardsforjustice.net*

3. A young woman came forward with information regarding aircraft hijackers who brutally beat passengers. She stated that she "felt strongly about justice being done." The team leader of the hijackers was returned to the U.S. and is imprisoned on air piracy charges.

4. A young woman, a student at a foreign university, witnessed a brutal assassination of a U.S. diplomat. Two attackers were placed in a foreign prison for life as a result of the information she provided. She received a reward.

In addition to a cash reward, personal protection is available. You and your family may be relocated to a safe location, and have an opportunity to start a new life, pay for a home, and educate your children. You will have acted with extraordinary bravery.

If you have information that prevents an international terrorist act or brings to justice persons who have committed one, make a confidential call to Rewards for Justice, at 1-800-USREWARDS. Outside the U.S., contact the U.S. Embassy or Consulate in your country.

Rewards work. Rewards do get paid. Thousands of people around the world can attest to it. They're alive because of them.

REWARDS UP TO $25 MILLION

CONTACT: Your local police, the FBI, or the nearest U.S. Embassy or Consulate. CALL: 1-800-USREWARDS. E-MAIL: mail@rewardsforjustice.net. *Rewards of up to $25 million, protection of your identity, and relocation of your family may be available for persons providing information that prevents an international terrorist act against U.S. persons or property or brings to justice persons who have committed one. To date, more than $8 million has been paid.*

Your call or e-mail will be kept strictly confidential.

REWARDS FOR JUSTICE
1.800.USREWARDS
www.rewardsforjustice.net

U.S. Department of State

Justice program.

The next day Beers appeared with Diane Sawyer on ABC's *Good Morning America*. During the interview, the Rewards for Justice radio spot was played:[10]

"Do you know a terrorist? Not long ago, this would have seemed like a ridiculous question. But not anymore. The United States government is offering rewards of up to $25 million for information that prevents an international terrorist act against U.S. person or property or brings to justice persons who have committed one."

Sawyer also read the headline for a print ad featuring a photo of the suspected leader of the 9/11 hijackers, Mohammed Atta. "He was spotted in Hamburg, Prague, Florida and Maine. And if someone had called us, his picture wouldn't be spotted in this ad."

At the end of the interview, Sawyer asked about Beers' broader plans for her new job of communicating America's ideals to the world. Beers' reply foreshadowed the Shared Values Initiative: "And then on to a long dialogue, an open dialogue with the rest of the Muslim world, hopefully."[11]

The Rewards for Justice ads did not escape the scrutiny of some who called them misleading and propagandistic. An Ogilvy executive who worked on the campaign said it was not without controversy. The ads asked U.S. citizens to be suspicious of their neighbors and report them to authorities—a request that did not sit well with some Americans.

Some leaders of the Arab-American community also were not pleased with the Mohamed Atta ad, saying it was misleading because, although the ad never mentions Atta's name, it bears his picture. The ad copy states that he wanted to learn to fly but didn't need to know how to take off and land. There was no record of Atta ever saying that, but, rather, the comment is attributed to another suspected hijacker.

The State Department responded that the ad is not about Atta specifically but about terrorists in general and what Americans could look for and what they may want to report regarding suspicious behavior.

But Fawaz Gerges, a professor of international affairs and Mideast studies at Sarah Lawrence College, told National Public

Radio listeners that "I don't buy that argument"[12] and said the ad was misleading and likely to aggravate Arab suspicions about U.S. motives and deepen anti-American sentiment.

Informational Pamphlets

The Office of Public Diplomacy and Public Affairs and its predecessor, the United States Information Agency (USIA), had long been known for distributing printed material about America for embassies to hand out to locals around the world.

When Beers was appointed, Secretary Powell made an often-quoted remark about her being able to do more than just hand out pamphlets. And Beers supervised the development of several printed pieces while she worked at the State Department.

A page from the Network of Terrorism booklet.

The Network of Terrorism was a sophisticated 26-page booklet that identified terrorist cells around the world and explained their role in the 9/11 attacks. Stocked by U.S. embassies, the brochure was printed in 36 languages and became the most widely distributed public diplomacy document ever produced by the State Department.

The booklet contained materials that embassy personnel could give to local media—a first for State Department publications. The booklet was also the first State Department publication to use full color, multiple graphics and sophisticated layout and design to enhance its effectiveness.

In the lead-up to the war in Iraq, Beers became responsible for developing communication pieces that explained to the Iraqi people the U.S. position against the Saddam Hussein regime. Beers' team prepared three booklets—*Iraq: From Fear to Freedom*, *Iraq: A Population Silenced* and *Iraqi Voices For Freedom*, which also was developed into a film containing voices representing Iraqis who desired changed in their country.

Iraq: From Fear to Freedom handbook

Cultural and Citizen Exchanges

The State Department also produced a 60-page book of 15 essays by famous American writers. Contributors to the anthology, called *Writers on America*, included American Pulitzer Prize winners Michael Chabon, Robert Olen Butler, David Herbert Donald and Richard Ford, American poet laureate Billy Collins, and Arab-American writers Naomi Shihab Nye and Elmaz Abinader.

The book, which was translated into dozens of languages, was distributed free of charge through American embassies worldwide in early 2003. Some of the essays also were posted on the Internet.

The anthology's contributors were recruited personally by the Bush administration. Some were paid a nominal fee for their work. In addition to contributing original essays, some of the poets and writers toured several countries giving readings and making speeches in an effort to further American interests.

The contributors were cautiously optimistic about the book's ability to change attitudes toward the United States. Collins noted at the time that having American writers touring around the Middle East gives the foreign press something to write about and may counterbalance the negative news about America that typically dominates their media. "It would have a positive and softening influence on things."[13]

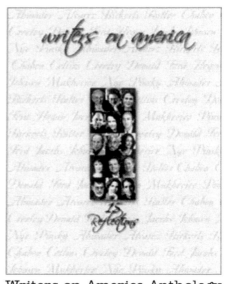

Writers on America Anthology

Beers did not direct the writers' program. It was part of an ongoing State Department focus after 9/11 to use culture to ingratiate international audiences. The program was similar to Cold War programs in which Soviet citizens would line up to see American art and dance or hear a famous American author speak in their country. But Beers did initiate a worldwide traveling exhibit of Joel Meyerowitz's photographs of the World Trade Center after the 9/11 attacks.[14]

International exchanges was another area of responsibility for Beers. She placed a high priority on these programs, believing that interpersonal contact with foreigners here or abroad could have a powerful impact on how others see America. On numerous occasions she spoke about her experiences with international visitors whom she had come to know through State Department programs.

In November 2002, she met 49 Arab women who came to the United States on a State Department grant to witness the election process. "They couldn't believe the fervor of the debate and then having it come to a common resolve the day after," Beers recalled.[15] She also spoke passionately about Afghan women visiting America and her hopes of sending American teachers to Afghanistan.

Beers actively promoted international journalist exchanges and invited a group of Middle Eastern journalists to interview American Muslims and send stories back to their countries. According to Beers, the freedom these journalists were allowed in the United States came as a wonderful surprise to them. Beers understood the power of personal interaction in effecting attitudinal change among people of different countries and cultures. She also knew that exchanges, while extremely effective, are costly and limited in scope. Mass media may not be as effective, but they are more efficient because they can reach millions with simple powerful messages quickly and inexpensively.

Additional Components
of the Shared Values Initiative

The Shared Values Initiative was a complete and integrated communication campaign using print and radio executions in addition to the television commercials or "mini-documentaries" that were described in Chapter 1. The print ads and radio spots mirrored the television commercials and were placed in tandem with the television spots during a 6-week campaign period running from late October to mid-December 2002 and coinciding with the holy month of Ramadan.

Shared Values Print Ads

The newspaper ads were essentially print versions of the television spots arranged in a vertical fashion featuring a shape and border reminiscent of traditional Islamic architecture. Each ad focused on one of the American Muslims featured in the television spots and began with a quote, which served as the headline. Below the quote was a dominant photo of the featured American Muslims taken from the television footage. The smaller body copy below the

SVI newspaper ads mirrored the television spots.

photo was similar if not identical to the copy in the television spots and told the story of the person's life in America.

As on television, the line "Brought to you by the Council of American Muslims for Understanding and the American people" was centered near the bottom of the ads. Unique to the newspaper executions, in very small type at the bottom of the ad, were details about CAMU, identifying it as a private, non-profit organization that "seeks to educate Americans and the world about the achievements of Muslims in America and throughout history." The newspaper ads also provided a toll-free phone number that could be used to receive a copy of the publication *Muslim Life in America* from CAMU.

According to McCann-Erickson media flowcharts dated September 30, 2002, newspaper and magazine ads were scheduled to run in Indonesia, Jordan, Kuwait, Lebanon, Malaysia, Morocco and Pakistan at a total cost of about $1.25 million. An Egyptian schedule was also planned but apparently never ran. A note on the media plan for Egypt indicated that the schedule was pending government approval.

As is common in the advertising business, a flowchart indicates a planned schedule, but there is no guarantee that the schedule actually ran as ordered. One McCann executive speaking on conditions of anonymity, described how staffers at the agency's Pakistani office made extraordinary attempts to physically transport copies of the SVI ads. In one case they hired a mule and rider to navigate a mountainous region in order to get the ads to a local newspaper.

There is some question whether the newspaper ads ran in Jordan and Lebanon because SVI television spots were refused there. The print ads ran in Indonesia, according to post-campaign research.

Table 3.1 details the newspaper and magazine titles, number of insertions, size and cost of the print advertisements that the State Department planned to run through its ad agency in each country.

Shared Values Radio

Radio commercials also were part of the SVI media campaign.

The radio spots were similar to the television ads in that they featured testimonials from American Muslims. The media strategy for radio was based on selecting listener profiles that matched the specified target audience and placing ads in programming environments that were not controversial, such as talk shows, religious programs, local music and news.

Little pre- or post-research is available on the radio schedule, but internal documentation indicates that SVI radio spots were scheduled to run in Indonesia on 50 stations in 29 cities, in Pakistan on FM 100 and FM 101, in Lebanon on Radio Orient and in Morocco on Medi 1 and Casa FM at a total cost of about $200,000.

Table 3.1
SVI Newspaper and Magazine Insertions

Country Medium	Newspapers	No. of Insertions*	Size of Ad	Approx. Cost in U.S. $
Indonesia Newspapers	Kompas, Republika, Media Indonesia, Pelita, Pikiran Rakyat, Suara Merdeka, Kedaulatan Rakyat, Jawa Pos, Waspada, Sumex, Lampung, Singgalang, Riau Pos, Benjarmasin Pos, Fajar, Koran Tempo, Serambi	5	Junior Pg Full Color	$405,123
Indonesia Magazines	Nova	3	Full Page	$17,787
	Tempo	3	Full Color	
	Sabili	2		
Jordan Newspapers	Al Rai	6	Full Page	$22,243
	Ad Dustour	4	b/w	
	Al Arab Al Yawm	2		
Jordan Magazine	Sharqiyyat	2	Full Page Full Color	$1,436
Kuwait Newspapers	Al Watan (70,000 copies)	12	40x5	$58,291
	Al Rai Al Aam (80,000 copies)	12	b/w	
Lebanon Newspapers	An Nahar	1	Full Page	$127,624
		4	Half Page	
	As Safir	2	Full Page	
		4	Half Page	
	Al Mustaqbal	3	Full Page	
		5	Half Page	
	Al Anwar	2	Half Page	
	Al Kifah Al Arabi	2	Half Page	
	Ach-Charq	2	Half Page	
	Al Liwa'	2	Half Page	
Lebanon Magazines	Al Afkar	5	Full Color	$28,100
	Ash-Shirah	5		
	Al Iktisad Wal Aamal	2		
	Al Hasna	2		
	Fayrouz	2		
Malaysia Newspapers	The Star (English)	3	Full Page/	$209,016
	New Straits Times (English)	3	Full Color	
	Mingguan Malaysia (wknds)	3		
	Utusan Malaysia (wkdays)	5		
	Berita Harian (wkdays)	8		
Morocco Newspapers	Al Ahdath al Maghribia	6	Junior Pge	$53,808
	Al Ittihad al Ichtiraki	6	Full Color	
	L'Opinion	6		
	Le Matin du Sahara	6		
Pakistan Newspapers	Dawn, The News, Nation Jang, Express, Nawai Waqt, Khabrain, Din Kawish, Ummat & Jasarat	20 / 14	Half Page Full Page	$330,909
Pakistan Magazines	Monthlies: Herald, Newsline, Weeklies: Family, Mag, Akhbar-e-Jehan and TFT	16	Full page	$19,594
* Ads spread equally over a six-week period of Oct. 28 to Dec. 13, 2002				

Source: McCann-Erickson

Muslim Life in America

A four-color magazine, titled *Muslim Life in America,* served as a companion piece to the SVI television spots and was distributed through U.S. embassies in selected Middle Eastern and Asian countries. The State Department's Office of International Information Programs (IIP) produced the magazine. Beers said in late 2002 that more than 300,000 copies had been distributed worldwide in nine languages, including English, Arabic, Russian and Thai.[16]

Muslim Life in America was produced with colorful pictures of American Muslims. Articles focused on the lives of successful and happy American Muslims and included other "facts" and demographic figures about Islam in America.

One issue included a map of the United States identifying the number of mosques by state (more than 1,200 total). An adjacent article, *American Mosques,* featured the photography and commentary of Dr. Omar Khalidi, a senior research scholar at the Aga Khan Program in Islamic Architecture at Massachusetts Institute of Technology. The article described the various types of mosques present in America and highlighted their importance to the American Muslim community. American mosques were also featured as part of a poster series released by the State Department.

Near the back of the magazine a page was devoted to quotes from President George W. Bush. Brief quotes concerning Islam and Muslims were reprinted under Bush's photo, including a greeting to Muslims across the United States on the occasion of Eid al-Adha, the Islamic festival of sacrifice.

The last page of the magazine sought feedback from the readers. The page, titled *Your Chance To Be Heard—What would you say to the American people?,* invited readers to send their thoughts, suggestions and questions to a post office box in Indonesia or to the State Department. It also provided an e-mail address for responses.

According to one of Beers' staff, the responses generated were overwhelmingly positive, although a few asked for help in obtaining a visa and immigrating to America. The staffer recalls receiving hundreds of feedback cards from throughout the Arab and Muslim world, but admits that no one took the time to formally analyze the responses. After Beers resigned, the response cards disappeared. A Freedom of Information request to the State Department for the response cards was still unanswered at the time of publication of this book.

Your Chance To Be Heard

What would you like to say to the American people?

Please write your thoughts, suggestions, and questions here:

Cut this card out and send it to either address below:

SURVEY RESPONSE
P.O. Box 1677
JKS 12016
Indonesia

or

SURVEY RESPONSE
IIP/T/CT/SA-11
U.S. Department of State
301 Fourth Street, S.W.
Washington, DC 20547

E-mail responses to: IIPTCT@pd.state.gov

A message from the Council of American Muslims for Understanding and the American People

Reader Response Card from Muslim Life in America magazine

In addition to the other support materials that accompanied the SVI television spots, speaker tours were arranged. American Muslims featured in the SVI spots traveled to the Middle East to speak to groups of citizens during and after the time the television spots aired. They included Abdul-Raouf Hammuda, owner of Tiger Lebanese Bakery of Toledo, Ohio, who traveled with his family to Lebanon at the expense of the State Department to talk about his life in America. Mr. Hammuda characterized his trip as very positive and said it provided an opportunity to expand the dialogue that was opened by the SVI advertising effort.

According to Hammuda, Lebanese journalists initially were very skeptical. As the conversation proceeded, they became more receptive, saying "We'll see what America does next." Hammuda acknowledged that his role in SVI was only a small part of a larger program and hoped it would be followed up with similar efforts by the U.S. government. "We [the United States] have a lot to give the world," Hammuda told us.[17]

Radio Sawa

While Charlotte Beers was operating her public diplomacy machine within the State Department and creating SVI to air on Middle Eastern and Asian television outlets, the Broadcasting Board of Governors (BBG) was seeking to expand U.S. government-sponsored broadcasting in the Middle East.

The BBG is a quasi-governmental board made up of private citizens from business and industry and is charged with overseeing Voice of America and other non-military government-supported international broadcasting. Board members believed America needed a "hipper" way to get its message across in the Middle East—"more MTV than NPR"[18]—which led to the creation of Radio Sawa.

Conceived before 9/11, the idea for Radio Sawa gained momentum after the terrorist attacks and captured a $35 million Congressional appropriation at the end of 2001. Radio Sawa, which means "together," first started transmitting in March 2002 from studios in Washington to the Middle East via satellite, shortwave and FM radio transmitters and the Internet.

Radio Sawa replaced Arabic Voice of America in the Middle East and was targeted to a younger audience. Featuring far less news than VOA, Radio Sawa's primary content is pop music, both American and Arab, with about 15 minutes of news each hour—and more if there is breaking news. Every few minutes the disc jockey breaks in between songs and reminds listeners, in English, that Sawa is "cool."[19]

Norm Pattiz, a media executive and founder of Westwood One radio network, served as chairman of the Middle East Committee for the Broadcasting Board of Governors. He has argued that the way to win hearts and minds in the Middle East is to appeal to young people who will become the future leaders, journalists and professors. However, some critics argue that the young people of the Middle East could also be future terrorists and could benefit from more serious broadcasting, news and analysis of American foreign policy, as was the case with the Arabic VOA. Responding to that criticism, BBG Chairman Kenneth Tomlinson told the *Washington Times*, "If you want your message to have impact in the Middle East, you have to be heard on a medium that they want to listen to."[20]

Nielsen ratings showed that Radio Sawa had high levels of listenership among young Arabs. In February 2004, Nielsen reported that Radio Sawa was a leading international broadcaster in the Middle East, with an average weekly listenership of 38 percent among adults (15 and older) in five key countries. More than three-fourths of Sawa's listeners rated the station's news and information as "somewhat or very reliable" according to a BBG report.[21] Older Arabs who were once regular *listeners* to VOA now tune to the BBC or Radio Monte Carlo.

Al Hurra

On Valentine's Day 2004, another U.S. government attempt to win hearts and minds in the Arab world went on the air.

Al Hurra, Arabic for "Free One," began its television broadcast by showing a series of windows being opened to symbolize freedom. Al Hurra is operated by the nonprofit corporation Middle East Television Network (MTN) and is financed by Congress through the BBG at a cost of $62 million for the first year—a considerable expense when compared with the $25 million that is spent by the State Department on all other public diplomacy outreach efforts in the Middle East.

Capitalizing on the success of Radio Sawa, the BBG launched Al Hurra to provide viewers with an alternative to Arab news stations such as Al-Jazeera. The commercial-free 24-hour satellite news channel broadcasts in the image of CNN, Fox or MSNBC and operates from studios in Virginia with facilities in Middle Eastern capitals such as Baghdad and Cairo. Its signal is carried to 22 countries via Nilesat and Arabsat—the same satellites used by the Arab-based stations. Al Hurra tries to compete with the Arab news stations, especially Qatar-based Al-Jazeera, by trying to counter anti-American news.

The Al Hurra staff consists of experienced broadcasters, producers and writers from Middle East television stations, including news director Mouafac Harb of Lebanon, who once worked for the Saudi newspaper *Al Hayat* and ABC news.

Al Hurra's promise to bring free and open news reporting to audiences in the Middle East was of course met with skepticism by many citizens in the region, who associate the U.S. government-owned media outlet with pro-Israel, pro-American propaganda.

Conclusion

After 9/11 the United States tried numerous new approaches to public diplomacy, many of which were discussed in this chapter.

Some of the new programs remain, but others ended almost as quickly as they were implemented. These new approaches have one common thread—they all use mass media and modern communication strategies to reach the "people," unlike traditional diplomacy that is one-on-one and targeted primarily to "elites."

This shift in approach by the State Department has not gone without criticism, particularly from seasoned diplomats and USIA old-timers, who believe marketing communication tools such as advertising, public relations and mass media are a waste of resources.

Some say the new approach is an international insult and cultural *faux pas* executed by an administration with little knowledge or concern for the outside world and controlled by corporate media types who have no business in matters of U.S. public diplomacy. A common argument is that these new approaches overlook the true crux of the problem—foreign policy, specifically the Arab-Israeli conflict.

Brandweek magazine editor Matthew Grimm expressed the sentiment of many opposed to the use of marketing strategies in the practice of public diplomacy when he wrote in 2003 that "marketing tools don't work in public policy." He concluded his article with a statement that seemed to be directed at Beers: "America is not a brand, and if you're thinking of it as such, get the hell out of government and go back to the corporate tower."[22] In the next chapter, additional reactions to Beers' style of public diplomacy are presented and analyzed.

But proponents argue that a large segment of international citizens can be persuaded by strategic use of the mass media and over time will develop a more positive attitude toward America regardless of what happens with global politics. In December 2002, shortly after the SVI campaign, Beers told the National Press Club that the United States must be proactive in getting its message out to the Middle East. "So, what about the elephant in the living room ... I'm referring to the hostility and distrust felt for the United States ... The counsel, 'Why don't we just wait until Middle East peace is resolved,' is tempting, but it's even more dangerous than silence."[23]

Chapter Endnotes

[1] For a complete transcript of Colin Powell's appearance on MTV visit http://www.state.gov/secretary/former/powell/remarks/2002/8038.htm. Retrieved on 28 October 2005.

[2] Barbara Slavin, "Sex, politics, but no rock 'n' roll: Powell talks openly with world youth," *USA Today*, 15 February 2002, p. B10.

[3] Jennifer Knoll, "U.S. hopes 'Hi' monthly will sway young Arab hearts and minds," *Jerusalem Report*, 8 September 2003, p. 7.

[4] Peter Carlson, "America's glossy envoy," *The Washington Post*, 09 August 2003, sec. *Style*, p. A01.

[5] "Arab youths wooed with US magazine," *BBC News* 18 July 2003. Retrieved from http://news.bbc.co.uk/2/hi//middle_east/3078063.stm on 13 September 2004.

[6] Matthew Lee, "US aims to win over Arab youth with glossy new magazine," *Agence France Presse*, 12 August 2003. Retrieved from Factiva on 5 November 2004 (Factiva Document AFPR000020030812dz8c002jt)

[7] U.S. Department of State, "Briefing on the Rewards for Justice Program," 13 December 2001. Retrieved from www.state.gov/secretary/former/powell/remarks/2001/dec/6844.htm on 30 August 2005.

[8] Ibid.

[9] Ibid.

[10] ABC News, *Good Morning America*, 14 December 2001. Broadcast transcript retrieved from LexisNexis on 15 August 2005.

[11] Ibid.

[12] Vicky O'Hara, "Profile: U.S. State Department defends an advertisement it placed in newspapers as part of the campaign against terrorism," *All Things Considered, National Public Radio,* 4 January 2002. Retrieved from Ebsco Host Database at http://search.epnet.com/login.aspx?direct=true&db=nfh&an+6XN200401042103 on 30 August 2005.

[13] Michael Z. Wise, "U.S. writers do cultural battle around the globe," *The New York Times,* 7 December 2002, p. B7.

[14] To see the exhibit on line visit http://www.911exhibit.state.gov/. Retrieved 31 October 2005.

[15] Charlotte Beers, Public lecture 6 December 2002, Southern Methodist University, Dallas, Texas.

[16] Ibid.

[17] Abdul-Raouf Hammuda, phone interview by author, 3 September 2005.

[18] Shane Harris, "Brand U.S.A.," *Government Executive* 35(14) (Special Issue, September 2003), p. 64.

[19] Ibid, p. 64.

[20] Donald Lambro, "Beaming up for Iraq's future," *The Washington Times,* 20 March 2003, p. A18.

[21] Broadcasting Board of Governors, "U.S.-funded radio and television make significant gains in Middle East despite anti-American sentiments." Retrieved from http://www.bbg.gov/printerfr.cfm?articleID=112 on 12 September 2004.

[22] Matthew Grimm, "Now the loser: Brand USA," *Brandweek, 44,* 20 October 2003, p. 19.

[23] Charlotte Beers, "Remarks to the National Press Club," Washington DC, 18 December 2002. Retrieved from http://www.state.gov/r/us/16269.htm on 3 November 2005.

Chapter 4

Reactions to the Shared Values Initiative

Reactions to the Shared Values Initiative and its use of advertising as a tool of public diplomacy were generally unfavorable. Many international and domestic news media, communication scholars, advertising executives, diplomats and government officials concluded that the campaign didn't work even though they provided little evidence to back up this conclusion. In contrast, former Secretary of State Colin L. Powell and former Syrian Ambassador Christopher Ross defend Under Secretary Charlotte Beers, SVI and the use of modern marketing tools for public diplomacy. In this chapter, Beers also responds to the critics and provides recommendations for public diplomacy.

Soon after the U.S. Department of State announced that Charlotte Beers was coming to Washington, columnists and critics began questioning whether an advertising executive could become an effective diplomat.

"[T]he Bush State Department appointee in charge of propaganda effort is a CEO (from Madison Avenue) chosen not for her expertise in policy or politics but for her salesmanship on behalf of domestic products like Head & Shoulders shampoo," wrote columnist Frank Rich of *The New York Times*. "If we can't

Charlotte Beers at a meeting while serving as Under Secretary of State

effectively fight anthrax, I guess it's reassuring to know we can always win the war on dandruff."[1]

"Her salary may be a governmental $133,700, but she lives like royalty," wrote *Time* magazine columnist Margaret Carlson. "Beers is close friends with Martha Stewart, dreams of being a country-western singer and favors body-length scarves, Jackie O sunglasses (indoors), and puffy bows the size of Uzbekistan around her neck."[2]

"America as brand assignment!" wrote columnist William Powers of the *National Journal.* "You could almost hear alarm bells ringing in newsrooms around the nation. Beers' use of advertising jargon hinted that we might be headed for one of those classic culture clashes between the very different worlds of New York business and Washington policy. She thrived in the Big Apple, but how would she fare in the brutal intramural combat of national government?"[3]

Many of the stories about her appointment called her the "Schmooze Queen of Madison Avenue" and speculated that she would be "selling America" like a consumer good. Few reports acknowledged that this was not a completely new idea. The government previously had employed advertising professionals to head international information services (see Chapter 2). Nor did the stories point out that Beers' herself said she was not really trying to sell America; rather, she was trying to start a dialogue with citizens in the Arab and Muslim world.

In September 2002, just before the SVI commercials were

broadcast, a senior fellow from the Council on Foreign Relations told *Advertising Age*, a leading industry trade magazine, that "nobody has felt the impact of anything she (Beers) has done."[4]

One of the few positive reactions came from *Advertising Age*. "Charlotte Beers knows how to crystallize that message and drum it home to her target audience," Rance Crain wrote in an editorial. "That's what advertising can do, and that's why all her years of experience will pay off in the most important assignment of her life."[5]

Powell Defends Beers

Secretary of State Colin L. Powell believed in Beers and her "branding" approach to public diplomacy and defended her throughout her tenure at the State Department.

"We are selling a product," he told a congressional committee before he appointed her to the post. "We need someone who can rebrand American policy, rebrand diplomacy."[6]

Later, after Beers was hired and journalists and others began to question her competence, Powell said, "She got me to buy Uncle Ben's rice. And so there is nothing wrong with getting somebody who knows how to sell something."[7]

In public speeches, Powell continued to support Beers and the idea of leveraging the communication know-how of the marketing and advertising community to strengthen public diplomacy.

Beers said Powell was one of her strongest allies while in Washington. But that support wasn't enough to quash the critics.

They continued to criticize Beers, even three years after the end of the SVI campaign and her resignation. Beers and her "failed attempts" at improving America's image were mentioned in media reports in fall 2005, when the new Under Secretary for Public Diplomacy, Karen Hughes, took office.

Reaction to Shared Values Initiative

Some politicians, government officials and journalists had good things to say about the Shared Values Initiative, but the overwhelming reaction was unfavorable from the beginning of the campaign until the end.

One of the earliest and most popular critical comments came from William Drake of the Carnegie Endowment for International Peace, who declared that "the notion that you can sell Uncle Sam like Uncle Ben's (rice) is highly problematic."[8]

Even before the campaign ended, some news media were concluding that the campaign was a flop. In November 2002, *Advertising Age* columnist Bob Garfield wrote, "This is no job for commercials."[9]

In March 2003, when Beers resigned from her position, many journalists and policy makers concluded that SVI had failed to achieve its goals. They made this declaration even though there wasn't enough empirical evidence to make a good judgment either way.

Anne Kornblut of the *Boston Globe* reported that "a controversial $15 million public relations campaign about Muslims in American life has yielded no measurable results in the Arab world."[10]

Marketing Week wrote, "No great surprise, then, that 'shared values' has failed to nudge the swingometer ... ."[11]

The Dallas Morning News called it "the not so hot 'Shared Values' ad campaign."[12]

And Margaret Carlson of *Time* concluded: "Uncle Sam is harder to sell these days than Uncle Ben's ever was."[13]

Some of the harshest criticism of SVI, however, came from the international press.

Reaction from International Media

The story of the U.S. government's $15 million "happy Muslim" ad campaign was reported in most major international newspapers, including the *London Times*, the *Courier Mail* in Queensland, Australia, and the Paris-based *Le Monde*. Stories also ran through the major international news agencies, including Agence France Press, the German Deutsche Presse-Agentur and U.S.-based United Press International and Associated Press.

Most stories covered the basic facts of the campaign, such as Beers' background in the advertising business, the cost to the U.S. taxpayers and some description of the spots. Many also talked about the Egyptian and Lebanese governments' refusal to accept the advertising. Some stories said the focus of the spots was off-target and blamed America's tarnished image on U.S. foreign policy, not on how Muslims are treated in America.

Even in countries with somewhat favorable attitudes toward the United States, SVI was dismissed. Singapore's *The Straits Times,* for example, characterized the campaign's launch in Malaysia as "a waste of time."[14]

As would be expected, the attempted airing of the SVI ads across the Muslim world prompted a strong reaction from media outlets. To no one's surprise, pro-Islamic and pro-Arab spokesmen came out strongly against the United States. These advocates used the ad campaign as a platform to register their disdain for U.S. foreign policy in the Middle East.

"This is so funny!" the Tunisian French-language newspaper *La Quotidien* wrote in a commentary. "Because what we understand from this campaign is that Americans just need a small cloth to polish their image, and that's it! In reality, Americans need much more than this to improve their image within the Arab-Muslim world."[15]

In Pakistan, SVI was parodied in the radical Muslim newspaper *Ummat*, which had a history of mocking U.S. Department of State messages. The paper ran its own version of the ads using the same graphic elements as the SVI print messages, but with different headlines and photos.

The first one, which ran on November 21, 2002, read, "I insisted on the freedom of my country and my religion. America killed me and left my five children orphaned."[16] It featured a photo of a dead Afghan.

Another ad in the same paper told the story of the hate-crime killing of a Muslim immigrant in Texas after 9/11—again mimicking the graphic look of SVI. Interestingly, Beers later interpreted these parodies as proof that the SVI message was getting through and that people were talking.

In Malaysia, *Berita Harain*, a pro-government English-language weekly, wrote:

> To even the impartial observer, this is a cynical campaign that insults the intelligence of the average Muslim. The Muslim world never has criticized America for its treatment of its Muslim community. It is the discrimination of the Bush Administration towards Islamic countries and their communities that has been criticized: The Palestinians, who have to endure oppression without any respite in sight; Iraqi citizens, who live under the threat of war; Malaysian students, who face gender discrimination in applying for their visas to the U.S. It is the foreign policy of Washington toward Islamic countries that is under scrutiny, not the treatment or the lives of American Muslims.[17]

Islamic Arabic-language newspaper *Attajdid* wrote: "Finally, the United States has become aware that its image is bad and ugly all over the world, particularly in the Islamic world. The entire world is feeling increasing hatred towards Washington, because of the U.S. arrogance and the injustice in the Middle East."[18]

Public relations firm Weber Shandwick Worldwide provided Beers' team a summary of media coverage of SVI from October 30 through December 12, 2002. The summary revealed SVI articles in newspapers, on national wire services and television networks around the world, including 14 articles in daily newspapers in Indonesia with combined circulation of more than 1.5 million and 12 articles in dailies in Lebanon with a combined circulation of 275,000.

Weber Shandwick also tracked "success stories" relating to SVI in other countries, including the widespread distribution of the State Department's publication *Muslim Life in America* among European and former Soviet countries. The agency reported no success stories in the Middle East other than in Kuwait, where the Secretary General and Public Diplomacy director of the Kuwait Student Union were "very enthusiastic" about the SVI spots.

According to the Weber Shandwick report, U.S. embassy officials were told that Kuwaitis were seeing the videos and "many are surprised that even in America Muslims are free to practice their faith and become important members of society."[19]

The State Department's Office of Research also collected and analyzed a sampling of foreign media reaction to SVI and published its findings in a report on November 26, 2002, titled, "U.S. image in the Islamic World: 'Policy' is the problem."[20]

The report analyzed 23 news articles from seven Middle Eastern and Asian countries from October 31 to November 26, 2002. The seven countries reviewed were predominantly Muslim nations— Egypt, Morocco, Saudi Arabia, Tunisia, United Arab Emirates, Malaysia and Pakistan. The report stated that Muslims and Arabs have extremely negative and distorted views of Americans and the United States.

The report also contained three key findings: (1) The negative image of the United States stems from U.S. foreign policy, especially in the Middle East regarding Israel and Iraq, and, thus, cannot be changed by words alone; (2) The SVI spots display American arrogance by targeting Muslim audiences and expecting them "to behave"; and (3) American Muslims are treated well in the United States, but Muslim visitors are "treated as suspected terrorists."

According to the report, Egyptian TV refused to air the ads because they were political advertisements. In Morocco the independent French-language weekly *Demain Magazine* criticized America's support of Israel against the Palestinians by saying, "Only when America (is just) ... can it win our sympathy, and then it will not need such expensive ads."[21]

London's pan-Arab paper *Al Hayat* suggested that the SVI campaign had been a complete failure and had caused incitement against U.S. foreign policy in Indonesia. Another *Al Hayat* columnist wrote that "the campaign comes in conjunction with beating the drums of the war against Iraq."[22]

A third *Al Hayat* piece was more favorable saying, "There is no doubt that the U.S. administrations' campaign is justified. Since the September 11 attacks, a wave of lies and conspiracy theories have swept over the Arab and Muslim world. The violations committed against Arabs and Muslims in the U.S. are unjustified, but still, they are not comparable to the massacre that caused them."[23]

Reaction from Academics

Domestic and international press coverage of SVI often included the expert opinion and reaction of scholars working at universities, research institutions and think tanks in America and abroad.

Mamoun Fandy, a senior fellow at the Baker Institute, was frequently quoted in the press. During an interview on the January 2003 PBS's NewsHour featuring SVI, he said, "I think this is wasted money."

The NewsHour host described Fandy as having served briefly as a consultant to the public diplomacy campaign "but now feels it has gone off course." During the televised interview, Fandy said, "The American campaign to inform the Muslim world about America has not only been just a failure, but it has contributed tremendously to anti-Americanism in the region."[24]

In a personal interview, Fandy told us that Beers and her team phoned him quite frequently to ask his opinions about using

American Muslims in the SVI ads. Fandy's strongest complaint was that Beers lacked understanding for the region and the people in the Arab and Muslim world. One example Fandy gave was the suggestion to feature famous American Muslims such as NBA star Kareem Abdul-Jabaar in the spots. Fandy thought the idea was ridiculous and would have been a huge mistake in the Arab world.

Fandy believed that problems associated with running the spots could have been avoided if Beers and the advertising agency had been more knowledgeable about the media landscape in the Middle East. "She did not appreciate that the countries in which she wanted to run ads were authoritarian and did not have free press systems like the United States," Fandy said.[25]

Despite his comments on PBS in 2003, Fandy was generally supportive of the idea of using mass media to communicate with audiences in the Arab and Muslim world. To reach Muslims in French-speaking North Africa, he suggested the French newspaper *Le Monde*, and to reach Muslims in English-speaking Arab countries, he suggested the BBC.

In January 2003, Youssef Ibrahim, a senior fellow at the Council on Foreign Relations, told *The Wall Street Journal*: "The ads were extremely poor ... It was like this was in the 1930s and the government was running commercials showing happy blacks in America. It is the policy itself we have to explain. You have to grab the bull by the horn, and the bull is 'Hey, here's our policy and there are good reasons for it,' instead of saying, 'Gee, there are a lot of happy Muslim people here.'"[26]

In February 2003, Rhonda S. Zaharna, associate professor of Public Communication at American University, told a hearing of the Senate Foreign Relations Committee that "instead of yielding a more positive American image, America's public diplomacy appears to have generated more anti-American sentiment."[27] Zaharna was critical of SVI for its use of impersonal mass media in "a region that values people and faces, not facts and figures."[28]

A resident scholar at the American Enterprise Institute also told

Advertising Age that Ms. Beers' notion of branding America "silly." "What we are facing with the Islamic world is nothing you could fix with advertising."[29]

Nancy Snow, assistant professor of Communications at California State-Fullerton and author of *Propaganda, Inc: Selling America's Culture to the World* (2002), has written several articles about Beers and the programs launched during her tenure. She agreed to communicate with us personally about SVI for the purpose of this book.

As a former Fulbright Scholar and United States Information Agency (USIA) staffer, Snow's initial reaction to Beers coming to the State Department was one of curiosity mixed with foreboding. She said she worried that Beers "would be eaten alive by the bureaucratic lifers in the foreign policy establishment."[30]

Snow's reaction to SVI was also mixed. She supports the idea of "telling America's story to the world" but thought the SVI message was off target. "Quite simply, global public opinion surveys from the Pew Global Attitudes Survey were showing that the world was already quite familiar with how well Muslim Americans were living," Snow said. "That wasn't the issue. The issue remained specific U.S. policy in the Arab and Muslim world, which as far as I'm concerned, Shared Values did not address."

Beers had Roper data to support her "shared values" approach, but apparently that message was not getting out to those who were vocal about SVI. This lack of awareness was evident when Snow said, "In fact, there was no evidence that the U.S. government and global publics had such shared values."[31]

Asked if she thought that advertising-type communication should be used in the future as a tool in public diplomacy, Snow said: "[The] U.S. is seen as the No. 1 propaganda nation in terms of promoting itself and reinforcing its popular and commercial image overseas, which makes global publics quite skeptical about U.S. government and industry intentions. Therefore, I would support advertising as one tool but make sure that such advertising is delivered in a pipeline that emphasizes public interest and public health messages, win-win solutions, and global civilian-based values, not national security values of the state."[32]

Reaction in Popular Media and Books

Simon Anholt, UK brand management expert and former international advertising executive, devoted several pages in his 2004 book *Brand America* to SVI.

Anholt contends that the main problem was that it came from the "to-know-us-is-to-love-us" school of public diplomacy. He argues that showing happy Muslims in America "isn't even a first good step in tackling the real worries of Muslims abroad about America's policies."[33]

Anholt also criticizes the emphasis on religious tolerance that could be interpreted in the Middle East as trivial treatment of Islam in America. And he was critical of television advertising because the vehicle symbolizes American popular culture.

But Anholt admits that his analysis is not the only "possible interpretation of the Shared Values Initiative," and it doesn't explain why the campaign may have failed.[34]

In the book *Bad News: The Decline of Reporting, the Business of News and the Danger to Us All*, former CBS news senior foreign correspondent Tom Fenton includes a few short and unflattering remarks about SVI and Beers. Fenton quotes the late ABC anchor Peter Jennings: "When I see the State Department come along and hire people out of advertising to improve the American image in the Middle East, I get really angry."[35]

Sheldon Rampton and John Stauber of the Center for Media and Democracy also blasted SVI in their Bush-administration critique, *Weapons of Mass Deception.* Rampton and Stauber criticize Beers' effort to "brand America," criticizing her alleged failure to address foreign policy concerns of the Arab and Muslim people. They write:

"By any measure, the Beers strategy was an abject failure."[36]

Three years later, in April 2005, Beers and SVI also were the target of ridicule on Comedy Central's *Daily Show with John Stewart.* "Muslims—there are a lot of them in the world ... problem is most of them hate us," one commentator said. "So President Bush has gone out of his way to change their minds. First he tried bombing them, but for some reason that seemed to make them angrier. Next he hired ad executive Charlotte Beers who made a commercial that was broadcast internationally about American Muslims who DO like us."[37]

Reaction from the Advertising Industry

One might have assumed that members of the advertising industry would have been supportive of SVI. Even if critical of specific aspects of the campaign, advertising executives could at least appreciate the persuasive role of mass media.

But several top U.S. advertising executives did not back the campaign.

"To call our country a brand is to denigrate it in people's minds," said Robert Keim, who was president of the Ad Council from 1966-87.[38]

Allen Rosenshine, chairman-CEO of BBDO Worldwide, defended the idea of branding and research in a February 18, 2002, commentary in *Advertising Age*. But he still argued that advertising was not the appropriate way to brand America.

"Detractors dismiss Charlotte Beers and marketing disciplines, but they're wrong ... it is wrong to dismiss branding as inappropriate just because it is mainly associated with commercial enterprises ... However, one valid criticism of branding America is that we cannot deliver it with advertising, certainly not in the traditional sense. Ads, commercials, slogans, jingles ... can indeed demean the effort."[39]

Reaction from the State Department

While the SVI campaign was running, the press frequently questioned the State Department about the commercials' effectiveness—about how they would be evaluated and if they were working.

But the State Department had difficulty explaining SVI and the evaluation program it had in place through McCann-Erickson advertising agency. In fact, State Department spokesman Richard Boucher often seemed uncertain in his responses to the questions.

During an October 30, 2002, press briefing, Boucher told reporters that the evaluation plan involving gauging "initial reaction from the newspapers, people we talk to, statements that are made and just [by] trying to get an idea of how it's playing as we go forward."[40]

On January 16, 2003, the day that *The Wall Street Journal* reported that the campaign had been suspended because it failed to register with Muslim audiences,[41] the press asked Boucher again, "How are you judging its [SVI's] success?"

His response remained uncertain and belied the difficulty that Beers' staffers had in communicating the strategic and evaluative criteria for the campaign:

> I think generally, the feedback we have had in terms of the way it has been discussed and debated, the kind of reaction we have had. I think they had done some focus groups already to see whether the message was getting across. It is just a means to sort of start to open minds, start to tell people a little bit about who we are and who they are and how that might work together.
>
> So I think we have generally felt that we have had that impact on the people we wanted to talk to—the people who do not know that much about it, who do not travel here, you know, four times a times year, who are not engaged with us already on the level of discussing policy. Now, that sort of measuring that is more depth, I think, that will come as this proceeds. But you cannot do all that right from an initial reaction because of the kind of message it is.[42]

Then Boucher was asked if he believed SVI to be a success. His response:

> I think, by and large, we believe that this was a very successful campaign. Remember what it was directed to do. It was directed to talk to people on a different level ... not to go through the policy debate, but to talk to people who are not part of that normal debate, tell them a little bit about who we are and what we stand for ...
>
> We feel it is quite successful in that regard ... We think there was an audience out there already of almost 300 million, maybe more, for these messages.[43]

Another reporter asked. "I just want to go back to public diplomacy really quickly and I don't want to split hairs, but when you say that you've opened minds through this campaign, do you have any sense whether or not you changed minds? Or just that people (laughter)—no, no, no—or just that people heard the message?"[44]

> We got a variety of reactions. The first thing was to make sure that people who we wanted to listen, to hear it, saw it and heard it. We are pretty sure that happened because of the feedback, because of the commentary, because of the tests we have been able to do.
>
> The second goal was to make sure that people were interested. And again, because of the feedback, because of the focus groups, because of that way it has been written up in various places, I think we can say with confidence that happened.
>
> The third was to establish some kind of identification with ordinary people in the Muslim world. Again, I think there is enough feedback and focus groups, people were interested in the message, people said that "yeah, I understand that there are certain things about them that are like us."
>
> And then now we really have to look a little more, I think, in more depth about the reaction. But, as I said, this was not convincing somebody of something as much as identifying the linkages, establishing the basis for more political discussions in the future.[45]

Boucher's vague responses and failure to present hard data no doubt contributed to the criticism of the program. At the same press conference, Boucher was asked if Beers would remain at the State Department. He said she was "doing great."

"Does the Secretary still maintain confidence in her?" a reporter asked.

"Absolutely. I do, too—and I work for her," said Boucher. This comment drew laughter from those in the room.[46]

In true governmental form, the State Department never openly criticized its Under Secretary Beers or her programs. To the press, State Department spokespeople were generally positive, although they sounded a bit unsure when speaking about SVI. And Secretary Powell maintained his confidence in Beers and her work.

Unofficially, however, many staffers at the State Department, especially those who had served long terms in the diplomatic corps, bristled at the idea of using advertising for public diplomacy purposes and were appalled by Beers' personal and business style.

"She's [Charlotte Beers] surrounded by cautious bureaucrats," said one official. "She cannot be productive and have those people around her. They're afraid to be controversial, afraid to be out there. That isn't her."[47]

After the SVI ads stopped, the State Department spoke positively about Beers and the campaign, saying that the communication plan had been "executed successfully" and that the ads had to be halted temporarily so that the mention of Ramadan could be removed. Officials also spoke publicly of launching the next stages of SVI, which were planned at the time of Beers' departure, according to internal State Department documents.

Powell said that efforts to reach a younger and broader audience would continue. In fact, after Beers left Washington in March 2003, SVI programs never resurfaced.

The State Department today generally refuses to comment when asked about SVI. Most of our requests for information have gone unanswered. We submitted a Freedom of Information Act request in

August 2005, but as of this writing none of the requested materials has been provided.

McCann-Erickson advertising staffers also were hesitant to speak about their role in SVI without permission from the State Department, which refused to grant that permission. Fortunately, we obtained much of the internal material just after Beers left Washington.

Reaction to Beers' Resignation

When Beers resigned after 17 months in Washington, the rhetoric became even harsher.

Insight magazine's J. Michael Waller reported in April 2003: "She couldn't do for Uncle Sam what she did for Uncle Ben's rice and so, after just 17 months on the job and on the eve of war, the advertising whiz who became Under Secretary of State for Public Diplomacy has quit, reportedly for health reasons. Her office is under fire from all sides for failing to inform and influence world opinion in the war on terrorism and the new theater of combat in Iraq."[48]

The advertising industry press was less critical. *Advertising Age* quoted her as saying that her public diplomacy programs were "misjudged" and that her time at the State Department had been a success.[49]

Wendy Melillo, *Adweek's* Washington bureau chief, wrote a favorable piece in June 2003 after Beers left. "The work was not a total failure: According to research the State Department shared with Congress, awareness of the campaign was up, and a shift in attitudes was beginning. Explain to me again how this is a bad thing?...Even some mid-level bureaucrats think advertising can help. It's a start."[50]

Although publicly State Department staffers were supporting SVI, privately some were highly critical of the program and no doubt ended up as "unnamed sources" in news stories. These and other "background" sources, as journalists call them, further undermined the SVI campaign and Beers' legitimacy.

According to a story in *The New York Times*, "many officials" in the administration were privately critical of the commercials, agreeing with Arab and Muslim officials that they were irrelevant to Muslim concerns about American policies toward Iraq and Israel. The same paper quoted an unnamed Congressional aide about Beers' departure and wrote that Beers had difficulty getting the message to hundreds of public affairs officers in embassies around the world and there was a "cultural problem" between her office and the bureaucracy she tried to influence."[51]

CNN.com reported that U.S. officials complained privately about Beers, saying "she is failing" and "she didn't do anything that worked."[52] CNN.com also quoted a government official as confessing that the administration waited until the fallout from SVI ended. "But we have been looking for an honorable exit for her for some time."[53]

CNN's Judy Woodruff reported immediately following Beers' resignation that "a U.S. official tells CNN that her departure was connected to problems that she encountered on the job. Critics complained that Beers spent a lot of money on slickly produced ads, but did not, the critics said, understand her target audience."[54]

Terry M. Neal, staff writer for washingtonpost.com, said that Beers' appointment was met with "snickers" and Washington's "important people questioned her lack of experience in political and diplomatic matters."[55] In contrast, one Congressman openly praised Beers when she left. An aide to Richard Lugar, R-Ind., chairman of the Senate Foreign Relations Committee, said, "Senator Lugar's view is that public diplomacy needs to be beefed up substantially and she brought a lot of new programs and ideas."[56]

Secretary of State Colin L. Powell also praised Beers upon her departure for her "incredible expertise."[57] "At a critical and stressful time for our nation," Powell told members of the Senate Foreign Relations Committee when she resigned, "she and her team sharpened our policy advocacy and took our values and our ideas to mass audiences in countries which hadn't heard from us in a concentrated way for years."[58]

Reaction from Government Hearings and Reports

In June 2003, Congress created a panel to study America's deteriorating global image.

In fall 2003, the bipartisan advisory panel, chaired by former Ambassador to Syria Edward P. Djerejian, released its findings in a report titled, "Changing Minds, Winning Peace: A New Strategic Direction for U.S. Public Diplomacy in the Arab and Muslim World."[59]

The Djerejian report's recommendations included spending more money on public diplomacy, which had dropped 50 percent in real dollars compared with the height of the Cold War in the 1980s.

The panel also called for a new position of "White House Director of Public Diplomacy" to serve as the President's "image czar"—a person who also would oversee the construction of libraries and information centers in the Arab and Muslim world and the translation of more Western books into Arabic, among other duties.

Other recommendations included increasing scholarships and visiting fellowships, upgrading the U.S. government's Internet presence, and training more Arab specialists, Arab speakers and public relations professionals to work in public diplomacy.

The Djerejian report devoted three pages in the appendix to SVI, which it called "well conceived and based on solid research."[60] However, the report said the delay in launching the program created problems and so did the resistance to SVI at some of the embassies, which in turn "may have contributed to the inability of the State Department to air the mini-documentaries on government television channels in key Arab countries."

The report called for an examination of the problems and incorporation of "host-country expertise and a better and swifter system for testing, contracting and approval."[61] It also provided a proposed timeline for a campaign such as SVI.

Perhaps the most interesting comment in the report was the panel's outright disagreement with "marketing experts who believed that advertising was not a good way to spread these messages."[62] The Djerejian report concluded that advertising is an appropriate tool for public diplomacy.

During the summer of 2004, the National Commission on Terrorist Attacks Upon the United States, known as the 9/11 Commission, released its report pertaining to the events, causes and recommendations concerning the events of September 11, 2001.

The independent, bipartisan commission made numerous recommendations to guard against future attacks, including a call for heightened emphasis on public diplomacy. While the commissioners did not address SVI directly, they may have alluded to it and programs like it when they wrote in the executive summary of the final report: "Communicate and defend American ideals in the Islamic world, through much stronger public diplomacy to reach more people, including students and leaders outside of government. Our efforts here should be as strong as they were in combating closed societies during the Cold War."

In response to the 9/11 Commission recommendations, the U.S. Congressional Subcommittee on National Security, Emerging Threats, and International Relations, chaired by Connecticut Congressman Christopher Shays, conducted a hearing August 23, 2004, to "assess the strengths and weaknesses of public diplomacy as a tool against future terrorist attacks."

Congressman Shays noted in his opening remarks that "words, not just weapons, fuel revolutions" and said that the 9/11 Commission found current public diplomacy efforts to be inadequate to meet the threat of terrorism. Shays also added:

"The Commission's call for reinvigorated public diplomacy adds urgency to the debate already under way over the appropriate mix of U.S. communication tools. Some say mass audience programming based on popular music and *other modern advertising techniques* (emphasis added) lack necessary depth. Others say the old, more academic methods targeting societal elites will not reach the larger body politic. The Commission calls for expansion of both approaches."[63]

The hearing contained three panels. The first panel included two of the 9/11 Commissioners; the second consisted of government representatives from the State Department, Broadcasting Board of Governors and the Advisory Commission on Public Diplomacy; and the third panel included two of the most powerful figures in the advertising industry, Keith Reinhard, chairman of DDB Worldwide and president of Business for Diplomatic Action (BDA), and Charlotte Beers.

While SVI was not included in the analysis, Reinhard appeared to allude to the program when he said to the committee at the outset of his speech, "It's not about making ads or 'selling' America. It's about actions."[64]

Reinhard used his time before the committee to discuss his private sector public diplomacy organization, Business for Diplomatic Action, and to stress that BDA efforts involved working with global marketers who represent America. Reinhard also emphasized that the U.S. government was "not a credible messenger" for effective public diplomacy messages and concluded his testimony time by outlining a post-9/11 communication strategy.

Beers was among the last to speak at the hearing. She had returned to Washington 18 months after resigning her post to address the congressional subcommittee about the weaknesses of current public diplomacy structure and to make her recommendations for future improvement. Her testimony contained five major points:

- Women are the agents for change in Arab/Muslim countries, and therefore we should empower the women and educate the young.
- Public diplomacy should be people-to-people, not government-to-government.
- Current public diplomacy work is hindered by its structure within government and is not well placed in the State Department.
- Public diplomacy employees lack the communication skills required to create persuasive and effective messages.

- The goal of public diplomacy should be mutual understanding and does not always have to include foreign policy at the front and center of every communication.

Beers acknowledged the contributions of the hard-working State Department public affairs people who skillfully engage with their governmental counterparts around the world. She stressed the need for public diplomacy to engage diverse audiences beyond the governmental elites. To do this, she said, requires skills in creating communication and programming designed not only to inform but also to influence.[65]

We, the authors of this book, also attended the hearing, because both Reinhard and Beers examined our research report on the effectiveness of the SVI spots before they testified. Although Reinhard had spoken out against programs like SVI, he and Beers had cordial interactions.

We also observed that acting Under Secretary of State for Public Diplomacy and Public Affairs Patricia Harrison was unable to respond to Congressman Shays' questioning about accountability and measuring the effectiveness of public diplomacy programs. We gave Shay's staffer a copy of our own research on SVI after the hearing.

Beers' Evaluation of SVI

From the beginning, Charlotte Beers has consistently maintained that the SVI campaign achieved its goals.

On January 16, 2003, the night that the State Department announced that the SVI spots had been discontinued, CNN's Aaron Brown asked Beers whether they had been effective.

Well, there are traditional ways of evaluating campaigns that ... go into broad-based, mainstream communication vehicles like television, print and radio, all of which we use. But the purpose of this effort is actually to create dialogue between the people of that country and this country. And the purpose of the dialogue is to talk about those things which we have in common. It's not meant to be a policy communication.

So ... did we start a dialogue and have we registered the message? In this case, the message was a story about religious tolerance in the United States. And we know this story is a very important one to those people. What we've learned so far is that they heard the message and they were quite surprised that there were mosques in the United States, and that there's a Muslim woman who's allowed to be a teacher and she could also wear her scarf with great comfort."[66]

A few weeks later, Beers also told the U.S. Senate Committee on Foreign Relations that 288 million people had been exposed to the SVI messages and that message recall in Indonesia was higher than that of a typical U.S. soft drink campaign.[67] She explained to the committee that qualitative research had revealed that the spots had achieved their objective by opening the minds of people who believed that Muslims in America were treated harshly.

One year after leaving Washington, Beers was interviewed by Bob Garfield on National Public Radio. "Nothing would be more dangerous than silence," she told him.

It's like asking Tylenol to be very quiet when people found out there was poison inadvertently put into their Tylenol packages. They went immediately to the air and every phase of communication to talk about what they were going to do, how it would be handled, and they won a huge round with the consumer groups. We do have some policies that are not popular, and that doesn't mean necessarily that we can make those popular, but we can certainly engage on many other fronts.[68]

In summer 2005, we interviewed Beers to see if her opinion of SVI had changed.[69] It had not.

Beers readily recalled research data for the television spots in Indonesia and continued to underscore that the overall objective of the campaign was not to sell America, but to open a dialogue with the

Muslim world.

We asked Beers whether she would have done anything differently.

"No, I wouldn't have done the program any differently." She added, however, that if she were to go through it again, she would navigate differently with respect to three "obstacles."

The first one involved the burdensome governmental approval system of public diplomacy messages. "I would have done the clearance process a little differently." The delay caused by the U.S. attorneys' insistence that the spots remove references to Allah took an additional four months. "So losing four months meant that that issue, which was more topical four months ago, was not as urgent."

Later in the interview, Beers noted that the delay became a plus by leveraging the timing with Ramadan. "There were lots of reasons why it was good to do it during Ramadan ... that's the time when everyone is watching television and they're not working."

The second obstacle Beers would have negotiated differently was "bringing the Near East embassies along earlier." The embassies were reluctant to embrace the SVI spots because "they had never seen an overt effort to talk to the people of the country, and they didn't want it because it just made their daily diet with their government officials more difficult."

In January 2003, she told CNN's Aaron Brown "I think that when you seek, as we are, almost for the first time, to reach past the government and the elites and talk directly to the people in the country, you are waging a bit of a communication war [with the authorities]."[70]

Indeed, the embassy officials became adversarial and, Beers told us, they said, "'You can't talk to our people directly.'" Beers regretted that the embassy resistance resulted in using pan-Arab satellite television, which in her opinion was "a lesser move."

Asked if she thought the embassy obstacle could be overcome and if messages such as SVI could ever be run on state-owned media in the resistant countries, Beers replied, "Oh, it just has to be begun and stayed with. And somebody who is making decisions on that just has to believe in it." She used Egypt as an example of a country with a sophisticated ambassador who was unwilling to encourage his government to support the campaign.

Beers believes that the U.S. government should be more insistent in the future when asking other countries to run pro-U.S. messages. "The answer has to be, 'then we'll try the next time and the next time and finally we'll get in' ... They (other countries) do it (run their ads) here (in the United States) all the time."

The third obstacle, she said, was the press. She specifically mentioned a negative article that ran in *The New York Times*, which "hit before anyone there had seen the documentaries." She also said some American Muslims actively sought to undermine the program in the media, including one man who initially provided feedback to the program and called it "wonderful."

"The irony is that I brought in a group of Muslim American people who were leaders in the country to help me develop this (SVI)," Beers said. "He was the one that was interviewed by all the television stations with a terrible critique. He's the very same person that sat in the room and said, 'this is wonderful.'"

Beers said she often was asked to explain why SVI did not deal with foreign policy. Why for instance, was there no mention in the ads about the U.S. government's stance regarding the Israeli-Palestinian conflict?

Beers emphasized that the campaign was designed to reach regular people in targeted countries, and not the elites. For regular citizens, the most important issues, according to the research, were faith, family, and education—not foreign policy. Foreign policy "was not even number six on their list ... regardless of what the governments think or what the highly sophisticated elites know about this subject."[71]

"The elites—the people who know everything about the United States—think we are talking about the wrong subject, because they know all the things about our country and its freedoms. What they don't know is what their own people think. They have no idea."[72]

Beers' Recommendations for Public Diplomacy

During an interview with us, Beers elaborated on two of her recommendations for public diplomacy.

First, she believes that the United States Information Agency should never have been placed in the State Department because the two agencies are incompatible. While embassy coordination is a necessity for public information programs to be launched, the embassies "should not have the power to completely block such programs,"[73] as they now are able to do.

Beers also feels strongly that the private sector must be used in public diplomacy. The private sector has much at stake in the fight against anti-Americanism and also possesses the in-country resources to make a difference among the people of other nations. Their words are potentially more believable to the people of other countries because they do not automatically represent U.S. foreign affairs, as do government spokespeople.

However, Beers believes that private corporations could not take over public diplomacy without the U.S. government's help in matters such as visa restrictions.

Does she believe there is a role for mass media in the future of public diplomacy? "I don't think there is any other way to do it,"[74] she said. She supports the use of U.S. government-sponsored media, such as Al Hurra and Radio Sawa and *Hi* Magazine.

Beers also emphasizes the importance of getting U.S. messages on local, private and state-owned television in the Middle East and Asia, including Al-Jazeera. Instead of using SVI-like paid advertising, Beers recommends full-length educational programs and documentaries for television stations overseas. She also suggests that the U.S. government sponsor training by American broadcasters for international television producers.

The Debate Continues

Although more than three years have passed since Beers left Washington, criticism of her and the SVI commercials can still be found in the popular press and on the Internet. This is unusual, considering the typically fleeting nature of the public's interest in any governmental program and the relatively low impact of SVI in terms of tax dollars spent and people reached.

On June 9, 2005, John M. McNeel, an advertising executive and board member of the nonprofit, private sector public diplomacy group Business for Diplomatic Action (BDA), wrote an opinion piece for *The International Herald Tribune*, titled "America, spare Arabs the spin." He criticized the idea of using advertising as a tool for public diplomacy.

"Although it may seem counterintuitive for an executive who has built his career helping clients invest their marketing budgets in ad campaigns to recommend that the U.S. government not spend taxpayers' money this way [on ads], I strongly believe that those funds can be more wisely used."[75]

BDA opposes the use of paid advertising for public diplomacy. However, the Council on Foreign Relations published a report in May 2005 arguing that future public diplomacy budgets should include money for mass media advertising overseas.[76]

U.S. Diplomats Take Up the Debate

U.S. diplomats have also taken up the debate over branding and the use of advertising in public diplomacy.

On the one side is John Brown, a former foreign service officer, who argues that Uncle Sam shouldn't be "branded" and that "the general consensus is that she (Beers) did little, if anything to 'move the needle' of world public opinion more favorably toward the United States."[77] Brown also writes on the Web site CommonDreams.org: "Her projects—including ... much ridiculed videos showing Muslims the happy life of their co-religionists in America— ... won't long be remembered. Beers's most lasting achievement will be seen in the negative."

On the other side of the debate is Joe B. Johnson, a recently retired senior adviser in the eDiplomacy Office at the State Department, who argues that SVI worked even though there were problems implementing the program. "After reviewing the 2002 Beers initiative, I am convinced that Shared Values' most important lessons have been hidden," Johnson wrote in the April 2005 *Foreign Service Journal.*[78]

"The fact is that the messages, which were researched and pretested with target audience members, actually worked when State was able to place them in foreign media. ... Beers failed, however, to anticipate the risk that her communication campaign might itself contribute to Muslim-American tension. When she revealed her plans for Shared Values to the press, that is exactly what happened. The campaign itself became an issue."

"Incoming public diplomacy executives can draw rich lessons from Shared Values," according to Johnson.

- First, research-driven persuasive communication is a valuable component of public diplomacy. Television and paid advertising are powerful channels of communication that should be available when they are needed.
- Second, coordinated action by different embassies is indispensable when publics reach across national boundaries, as they usually do.
- Third, our PD officers need both the tools and the culture of measuring audiences and results. Formal evaluation is the final necessary step to any professional campaign.

Johnson also concluded that "to take public diplomacy to the next level," the State Department must seek expertise from the private sector.

The articles by Brown and Johnson are reprinted in their entirety in Appendix B and C, respectively, of this book.

Reaction from Ambassador Christopher Ross

Although most current State Department employees would not talk with us, some former employees and diplomats gave us their opinions. One was former Ambassador to Syria Christopher Ross, who worked closely with Beers on SVI. Others who commented asked not to be identified.

In July 2005, Ross, who continues to work at the State Department but not in public diplomacy, told us that he holds generally favorable opinions of Charlotte Beers and the Shared Values Initiative campaign. He praised Beers for drawing on her previous experience in advertising and for her insights on the use of television to reach Arab and Muslim audiences.

Ross characterized SVI as "successful in certain Muslim countries and less successful in Arab countries."[79] Ross agreed with Beers' conception of the SVI spots, which was to counter the idea in the Arab and Muslim world that America was anti-Islamic. Research showed that this belief was fueled after 9/11 by the announced "war on terror."

But Ross said SVI suffered from two significant problems.

The first was the four-month production delay caused by the Justice Department's concern that the content constituted advocacy of Islam.

The second problem was the political resistance from the Arab world. He explained that both weaknesses were related. The SVI campaign, which was conceived in late 2001, took more than 12 months to produce and air. What happened in the interim, according to Ross, was that the focus in the Arab world shifted away from concern about anti-Islamic feelings and the treatment of Muslims in America to the Palestinian/Israeli crisis and looming conflict with Iraq.

The SVI spots did not address either of these subjects. According to Ross, this caused the Arab world to label SVI as an irrelevant campaign. Ross added that the Arab governments did not want to portray themselves as collaborating with the United States during very difficult political times, so most countries refused to run the ads. This caused the campaign to be relatively unsuccessful in the Arab world, while it still played fairly well in non-Arab countries, such as Indonesia.

We also asked him why so many people believe SVI was a failure.

"It was never conceived to be an on-going thing over months and years," Ross said. "It was a multi-media campaign that was to run for a distinct amount of time, after which we were move on to other things. It isn't accurate to say the State Department shifted gears. The campaign came to an end—it coincided with all of this criticism coming out from the Arab world, so it was somehow interpreted that in the face of that criticism the State Department decided to pull the plug ... But there was no conscious decision at State which said 'this thing isn't working, let's stop.'"[80]

Ross also said Beers' Madison Avenue roots made many people in the diplomatic world uncomfortable, and, therefore, it was easy for them to say that nothing she did had worked.

Asked if he believed a program similar to SVI could work in the future, he replied, "It isn't an impossible task. On its TV aspect, there are many more stations since 9/11, and they are scrambling for programming. What we did in the form of paid advertising with SVI could be done for free in the form of program documentaries."

Ross said many of the programs and ideas initiated by Beers at the State Department continue to operate.

[T]he fact is that many things she did were relevant and have affected how we do public diplomacy today. Such as getting to know your audience, knowing its concerns, developing a marketing-oriented approach to the audience, making an effort to craft the messages in light of those concerns so that they are meaningful, and measuring your efforts through polling.

Charlotte Beers brought a great deal of focus on moving from market to message to measurement. She focused people's attention on the central role of television—that was a great contribution. She established *Hi Magazine* ... . I myself think her contribution to the State Department was a very positive one, although the campaign that she has become known for to the exclusion of almost anything else had its problems.[81]

Reaction from Colin Powell

In a brief interview with us on September 6, 2005, Powell continued to defend Beers and remained supportive of her work despite the criticism.

"Here was this person, and they said, 'she sold Head and Shoulders dandruff shampoo. What does she know?' And I said, you bought the shampoo, didn't you?"

About SVI, Powell contended that the campaign "had some merit," but that "the timing was bad. We were going to war with Iraq. My Arab advisers told me it didn't play well."[82]

Conclusion

Reaction to the Shared Values Initiative was unfavorable from the beginning to the end of the campaign. Politicians, scholars, government officials, professional communicators and the domestic and international press were generally critical, and many concluded that the campaign did not work. Only a handful of diplomats, including Colin Powell and Christopher Ross, supported Charlotte Beers' campaign.

A number of theories have been offered to explain the negative response. One is that the Beers underestimated the extent to which the campaign itself would become news. Another is that foreign ambassadors failed to support the effort. And a third is that the State

Department failed to issue a formal statement about the effectiveness of the campaign and to provide stronger backing for Beers.

Whatever the causes of the negative assessments, one of the interesting aspects is that many critics concluded that the campaign did not enhance America's image even though they had little evidence to support that conclusion. In the next two chapters, we present the results of empirical research into the question of whether the Shared Values Initiative worked.

Chapter Endnotes

[1]Frank Rich, "Journal: How to lose a war," *The New York Times,* 27 October 2001, sec. A, p. 19.

[2]Margaret Carlson, "Can Charlotte Beers sell Uncle Sam? Margaret Carlson on a former ad whiz's new gig," *Time On-line edition,* 14 November 2001, retrieved from www.time.com/time/nation/article/1,8599,184536.html.

[3]William Powers, "Brand of the free," *National Journal,* 17 November 2001, p. 3577.

[4] Ira Teinowitz, "Beers draws mixed review after one year," *Advertising Age,* 23 September 2002, p. 3.

[5]Rance Crain, "Selling the Idea of Freedom the Most Important Assignment for Beers," *Advertising Age,* 5 November 2001, p. 12.

[6]House Budget Committee, "U.S. Representative Jim Nussle (R-IA) holds hearing on State Department fiscal year 2002 Budget Priorities," 15 March 2001. Retrieved from FDCH Political Transcripts on LexisNexis.

[7]Hearing of the Senate Foreign Relations Committee, "International campaign against terrorism," 25 October 2001. Retrieved from Federal News Service through LexisNexis.

[8]Alexandra Starr, "Charlotte Beers' toughest sell," *Business Week,* 17 December 2001, p. 56.

[9]Bob Garfield, "State Department effort asks the impossible of advertising," *Advertising Age,* 25 November, 2002, p. 33.

[10]Anne Kornblut, "Problems of image, diplomacy beset United States," *Boston Globe,* 9 March 2003, p. A25.

[11]"Beers bombs in the Middle East," *Marketing Week,* 13 March 2003, p. 3.

[12]G. Robert Hillman, "White House Public-Relations Office Aims to Tilt Global Spin," *The Dallas Morning News,* 19 March 2003, p. 19A.

[13]Carlson, "Can Charlotte Beers sell Uncle Sam?"

[14]Leslie Lau, "U.S. Muslim ad drive on Malaysian TV 'a waste of time,'" *Straits Times Singapore*, 6 November 2002. Retrieved from http://www.straitstimes.com.sg/asia on January 30, 2003

[15]Quoted in U.S. Department of State, Office of Research, "U.S. image in the Islamic world: Policy is the problem," Ben Goldberg (ed), 26 November 2002. Retrieved from http://www.globalsecurity.org/military/library/news/2002/11/mil-021126-wwwh21126.htm on 28 October 2003.

[16]Weber Shandwick Worldwide, "Success stories on Shared Values effort," 12 December 2002, unpublished internal State Department memorandum.

[17]State Department, Office of Research, "U.S. image in the Islamic world: Policy is the problem."

[18]Ibid.

[19]Weber Shandwick Worldwide, "Success stories on Shared Values effort."

[20]The report is available at www.globalsecurity.org/military/library/news/2002/11/mil-021126-wwwh21126.htm.

[21]State Department, Office of Research, "U.S. image in the Islamic world: Policy is the problem."

[22]Ibid.

[23]Ibid.

[24]"Public Diplomacy," Online NewsHour Transcript, 21 January 2003. Retrieved from www.pbs.org/newshour/bb/media/ janjune03/diplomacy_1-21.html on 6 February 2003.

[25]Mamoun Fandy, telephone interview with authors, Tulsa, OK, 3 September 2005.

[26]Vanessa O'Connell, "U.S. suspends TV ad campaign aimed at winning over Muslims," *Wall Street Journal,* 16 January 2003, p. A1.

[27]R. S. Zaharna, "American public diplomacy and the Islamic and Arab world: A communication update & assessment," Testimony before the Senate Committee on Foreign Relations, 27 February 2003. Retrieved from http://foreign.senate.gov/testimony/ 2003/ZaharnaTestimony030227.pdf. on 2 November 2005.

[28]Rhonda S. Zaharna, "The network paradigm of strategic public diplomacy," *Foreign Policy in Focus* (April 2005). Retrieved from http://www.fpif.org/fpiftxt/970 on 2 November 2005.

[29]Ira Teinowitz, "Beers draws mixed review after one year," *Advertising Age,* 23 September 2002, p 3.

[30]Nancy Snow, email interview by the authors, 29 August 2005.

[31]Ibid.

[32]Ibid.

[33]Simon Anholt and Jeremy Hildreth, *Brand America: The Mother of All Brands* (London: Cyan Books, 2004), p. 142.

[34]Ibid, p. 144.

[35]Tom Fenton, *Bad News: The Decline of Reporting, the Business of News and the Danger to Us All* (New York: Harper Collins, 2005), p. 140.

[36]Sheldon Rampton and John Stauber, *Weapons of Mass Deception: The Uses of Propaganda in Bush's War on Iraq* (New York: Jeremy P. Tarcher/Penguin, 2003), p. 34.

[37]Ed Helms, "What's it gonna take?" *The Daily Show with John Stewart on Comedy Central,* 13 April 2005.

[38]Quoted in Powers, *Brand of the Free,* p. 3578.

[39]Allen Rosenshine, "Now a word from America," *Advetising Age,* 18 February 2002, p. 15.

[40]State Department Daily Press Briefing, Richard Boucher, Spokesman, 30 October 2002. Retrieved from http://www.state.gov/r/pa/prs/dpb/2002/14805.htm on 1 November 2005.

[41]O'Connell, "U.S. Suspends TV Ad Campaign," p. A8.

[42]State Department Daily Press Briefing, Richard Boucher, Spokesman, 16 January 2003. Retrieved from http://www.state.gov/r/pa/prs/dpb/2003/16717.htm on 1 November 2005.

[43]Ibid.

[44]Ibid.

[45]Ibid.

[46]Ibid.

[47]Quoted in Powers, "Brand of the free," p. 3578.

[48]J. Michael Waller, "U.S. not getting message out," *Insight on the News,* Vol. 19. (1 April-14 April 2003), pp. 26-28.

[49]Ira Teinowitz, "Beers: State Dept. program misjudged," *Advertising Age,* 10 March 2003, p. 3.

[50]Wendy Melillo, "The peace brokers: Ad execs can still help American diplomacy in the Arab world," *Adweek,* 23 June 2003, p. 21.

[51]Steven R. Weisman, "Powell aide quits position promoting U.S.," *The New York Times,* 4 March, 2003, p. A12.

[52]"Bush's Muslim propaganda chief quits," *CNN.com,* 4 March 2003, Retrieved from http://cnn.com/2003/US/03/03/ state.resignation/index.html on 01 November 2005.

[53]Ibid.

[54]As quoted in Terry M. Neal, "Image problem remains after departure," *Washingtonpost.com,* 6 March 2003.

[55]Ibid.

[56]Ira Teinowitz, "Charlotte Beers to resign from State Department," AdAge.com, 3 March 2003, Retrieved from http://www.adage.com/news.cms?newsID=37278 on 4 March 2003.

[57]State Department Daily Press Briefing, Richard Boucher, Spokesman reading Secretary Powell's remarks, 3 March 2003. Retrieved from http://www.state.gov/r/pa/prs/dpb/2003/18144.htm on 1 November 2005.

[58]Ibid.

[59]Edward P. Djerejian, Chairman, Report of the Advisory Group on Public Diplomacy in the Arab and Muslim World, *Changing Minds, Winning Peace: A New Strategic Direction for U.S. Public Diplomacy in the Arab and Muslim World,* 1 October 2003. Retrieved from http://www.publicdiplomacy.org/23.htm on 2 November 2005.

[60]Ibid., p. 72.

[61]Ibid., p. 72.

[62]Ibid., p. 72.

[63]Christopher Shays, "Shays statement for hearing on 9/11 Commission Recommendations on Public Diplomacy," 23 August 2004. Retrieved from http://www.house.gov/shays/news/2004/august/augpub.htm on 1 November 2005.

[64]Keith Reinhard, Testimony to the House Subcommittee on National Security, Emerging Threats and International Relations, 23 August 2004. Retrieved from www.aaf.org/news/pdf/bdatestimony.pdf on 2 November 2005.

[65]Charlotte Beers, Testimony to the House Subcommittee on National Security, Emerging Threats and International Relations, 23 August 2004. Retrieved from reform.house.gov/ UploadedFiles/CBTestimony_Aug2304.pdf on 3 November 2005.

[66]Aaron Brown, "Charlotte Beers," Interview on CNN's *NewsNight,* 16 January 2003, aired at 10 p.m. EST. Retreived from INK "http://www.state.gov/r/us/16735.htm on 3 November 2005.

[67]Charlotte Beers, Testimony to the Committee on Foreign Relations, 27 February 2003. Retrieved from retrieved from foreign.senate.gov/testimony/2003/BeersTestimony030227.pdf

[68]Bob Garfield "Selling America," NPR radio interview with Charlotte Beers, 26 March 2004. Retrieved from http://www.onthemedia.org/transcripts/transcripts_032604_selling.html on 3 November 2005.

[69]Charlotte Beers, phone interview by authors, 5 July 2005.

[70]Beers, interview on CNN's *NewsNight,* 16 January 2003.

[71]Beers, interview on CNN's *NewsNight* 16 January 2003.

[72]Beers, phone interview by authors, 5 July 2005.

[73]Beers, phone interview by authors, 5 July 2005.

[74]Ibid.

[75]John M. McNeel, "America, spare Arabs the spin," 9 June 2005, *International Herald Tribune,* p. 8.

[76]Craig Charney and Nicole Yakatan, "*A New Beginning: Strategies for a More Fruitful Dialogue with the Muslim World,*" (Council on Foreign Relations, Inc.: New York, 2005).

[77]John Brown, "Don't brand the U.S. Uncle Sam: The backlash against Charlotte Beers' American branding," posted on *CommonDreams.org* 13 December 2004. Retrieved from http://www.commondreams.org/views04/1213-24.htm on 1 November 2005.

[78]Joe B. Johnson, "Public Diplomacy: What have we learned?" *Foreign Service Journal,* (April 2005), pp. 13-14.

[79]Christopher Ross, phone interview by authors, 28 July 2005.

[80]Ibid.

[81]Ibid.

[82]Colin Powell, interview by author, Dallas, Texas, 6 September 2005.

Chapter 5

Did Shared Values Work?
The Post-Campaign Study

Most U.S. and foreign journalists, advertising executives and government officials concluded the Shared Values Initiative campaign didn't work. But what did the post-campaign research show? This chapter answers that question first by examining how message effects are measured among target audience members and second by looking specifically at the SVI post-campaign tracking study that was conducted in Indonesia in late 2002. Audience data and SVI-related Web site visits from other targeted countries also are presented and analyzed.

Much of the early reaction to the Shared Values Initiative (SVI) was anecdotal in nature and understandably so. In the absence of survey or experimental data to measure the advertising campaign's success, journalists who covered the new and unprecedented public diplomacy initiative had to rely on interviews and person-on-the-street quotes to describe reaction.

Although anecdotes often are used to illustrate general trends and findings, they can also mislead if they are not representative of the population or phenomena under study. A good example of this problem is the CNN report mentioned earlier that quoted an Indonesian cab driver's reaction to the SVI commercials: "I don't know what the point of this is. If they are selling something, what is it?"[1] In this case, an unscientific sampling of one cab driver can be easily misinterpreted as reflecting the opinions of an entire population of people who saw the spots. To be fair, CNN reports of SVI contained interviews with other people who reacted more positively to the spots, but these person-on-the-street interviews also may not reflect the views of the entire population.[2]

Good research is needed to accurately assess the impact of an advertising campaign. And for most campaigns, this can take several weeks or months.

Unfortunately, when the SVI ads began running, the news media wanted an instant answer to the question of how effective they were. At that point, the State Department did not have good answers. Nor did it do a good job in explaining that the SVI spots were only one small part of a multi-dimensional communication campaign designed to open a dialogue with average citizens in the Arab and Muslim world about life in America. The goal was not to change opinions. It was to start a dialogue.

From the beginning, most journalists had unrealistic expectations for the relatively modest advertising campaign, and those who clung to these expectations were disappointed.

Judging Advertising

One need only mention the subject of advertising at a cocktail party to demonstrate how willing most people are to express an opinion about the effects of advertising.

Many people quickly pass judgment about how brilliant, or misguided, a creative effort might be. Although the same people are unlikely to second-guess a decision by a NASA engineer involving the Space Shuttle or even a plumber about repairing the kitchen sink, many people regularly transform into armchair advertising critics at will. This is the case even though assessing the effects of an advertising campaign often requires years of formal education and sophisticated scientific research methods.

At least two factors explain why advertising is the subject of relentless public scrutiny and judgment.

First, advertising by its nature is a very public enterprise, and many people are exposed to it whether they are the intended target market or not. Much criticism of advertising comes from those who are not in the designated audience. Research has shown that people who are exposed to but are not in the market for such products as denture adhesives, life insurance or other products they don't buy often consider such advertising annoying because it doesn't apply to them. In some cases, viewers have objections to the very fact that a particular product is being advertised at all—such as male sexual dysfunction prescription drugs or alcoholic beverages.

Second, consumers are rarely, if ever, privy to either the intended strategy of the ad, or how well the ad actually performed in the marketplace. That, of course, is only for the advertiser to know, and typically results are not shared with the public or competitors.

In the case of SVI, the advertiser was the State Department—a very visible public institution funded by the American taxpayers and whose actions are covered daily by the mass media. Charlotte Beers understood the importance of communicating her public diplomacy strategies with the American people and was willing to explain the objectives behind the SVI campaign to the press, Congress and others. She came from the advertising industry where she directed advertising specialists who had experience in the art and science of persuasion. But her staff at the State Department was far less competent at such matters and in some cases unwilling to communicate the goals of SVI with outsiders.

In fact, her staff of long-time diplomats, foreign service officers, public affairs personnel and other State Department employees had little knowledge of the principles of mass communication. This situation was complicated even more by the fact that the State Department had inherited the public diplomacy functions from the former United States Information Agency (USIA), and some employees were forced into new jobs for which they were not well-suited.

Beers said she had to spend at least part of most meetings with her staff explaining the basics, or as she called it, "Communication 101." To overcome this challenge, Beers implemented training sessions for some public affairs officers and embassy personnel to help them learn communication fundamentals and apply that knowledge to improving public diplomacy.

Explaining the objectives and effectiveness of a mass media communication campaign to the press is never easy. This is especially true because most journalists do not have formal education or training in social science research methods.

The situation with SVI was complicated even more because the press corps adopted a cynical tone early on, often referring to Beers' appointment as "Madison Avenue coming to Foggy Bottom." They used clever quips like "Can she sell Uncle Sam like she sold Uncle Ben's?" Such rhetoric made for good headlines, but it did little to explain SVI or its effectiveness.

According to members of Beers' team, the press often refused to listen and report what Beers was saying. Beers maintained that improving attitudes toward America was a lofty goal that SVI could not achieve. She repeatedly stated that her objective was simply to "start a dialogue" with people in Muslim countries by informing skeptical audiences in the Middle East and Asia that America and the Muslim world share common values.

Beers hoped that SVI could persuade viewers to be more aware, open and accepting of America by dispelling myths about the treatment of Muslims. Put another way, Beers saw SVI as the first step toward "winning hearts and minds," which would be followed by additional public diplomacy activities such as American speaker tours and international citizen exchanges within the targeted countries.

However, this information about campaign objectives as well as the post-campaign evaluation research was largely ignored.

"Sometimes I felt that if I heard someone say 'selling America' one more time, I was going to scream!" one former Beers' staffer said.[3]

Some of the blame can be attributed to poor communication from State Department spokespersons not trained in advertising and social scientific research methods (see Chapter 4 for more details). But some reporters who were given an accounting of the goals and effects of the campaign refused to publish that information and instead concluded that the campaign was a failure.

Advertising 101

Most people don't associate advertising with scientific research and theory. They often view it as entertainment at best and hucksterism at worst.

But advertising draws heavily from the social scientific disciplines of persuasion, communication, social psychology and marketing. Although a relatively new area in the social sciences, advertising as an academic discipline is supported by decades of empirical research and theory construction. Research and theory guide the advertising practices that result in the commercials, billboards and other ads that consumers see on a daily basis.

Advertising is usually defined as paid media content whose intent is to inform or influence people or organizations to buy a product or service. This as well as other definitions of advertising contain at least six elements:

1) Advertising tends to be *nonpersonal*, which means that it is carried via mass media as opposed to personal communication that takes place between individuals.
2) Advertising is usually *one-way* because of the nature of traditional mass media delivery; however, with new media technologies such as the Internet, advertising is developing certain aspects of two-way communication.

3) Advertising is a *planned message* for which an
4) *identified sponsor pays* the
5) *mass media* to distribute. This suggests that advertising communication is not ad hoc, but rather is controlled by the sender.
6) Most importantly, when advertising works, *it affects knowledge, attitude and behavior*. Advertising is, by definition, persuasive communication.[4]

In its simplest form, advertising is a form of communication, which involves the flow of a message from the sender to a receiver through some type of medium.[5] There is, of course, the potential of interference with the message (noise). The receiver may provide feedback to the sender, creating a continuous loop (see Figure 5.1).

In the case of advertising, the sender is the sponsoring company or brand advertiser, the receiver is the target audience, the message is the ad and the medium might be television, newspaper or some other vehicle.

In the case of the SVI commercials, the sender was the U.S. government and the receivers were the audiences in predominantly Muslim countries. The message is contained in the SVI spots, which were carried over the medium of television.

Persuasion theory helps explain how different aspects of the communication model may be altered to improve the chances of effective persuasion taking place.

Persuasion Theory

Persuasion is usually defined as attitude change resulting from exposure to information from others.[6]

The study of persuasion goes back to Plato and Aristotle. For the Greeks and Romans, persuasion could take the form of an argument, debate, discussion or public speech effectively arguing a

Figure 5.1

Communication Model

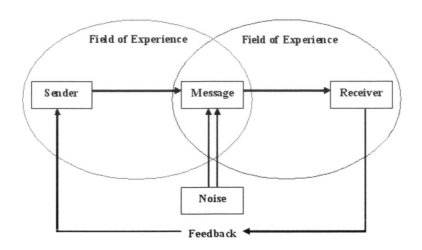

point of view. Techniques required for effective persuasion were honed, practiced and applauded in the public arena. Much of America's government and legal system is derived from these ancient societies, which had great respect for public discourse and informed discussion—the tools of persuasion.[7]

When applied to advertising, the goal of persuasion is to change consumers' attitudes toward a particular product, brand, person or idea that ideally will lead to buying the product, voting for a political candidate or accepting an idea, such as "only you can prevent forest fires."[8]

Effective persuasive communication is elusive and difficult to achieve. Researchers have studied the idea extensively over the last half-century. The overview that follows is, of course, very abbreviated and stresses only selected elements of persuasion research. In the context of SVI, the concepts will be revisited in the final chapter.

Carl Hovland

During the 1940s, Carl Hovland, a Yale psychology professor, attempted to uncover the "magic keys of persuasion."[9]

During World War II, he and his colleagues conducted research on U.S. soldiers, assessing the effectiveness of messages designed to increase knowledge about the war and motivation to fight (see Chapter 2). After the war, Hovland continued looking for the perfect set of conditions and combinations of variables that would allow persuasion to take place without fail.

Of course, he was never able to achieve this goal. Human behavior is very complex and sometimes unpredictable. He did, however, make some important discoveries that continue to serve as the basis of understanding how persuasion works.

A few are reviewed here—especially those relevant to SVI. They include source credibility, sleeper effect, one-sided versus two-sided messages and audience personality factors. The two-step flow of communication theory is also discussed.

Sender Variables

One of the most important elements influencing the effectiveness of a persuasive message is the credibility of the sender. If the sender is not perceived as being credible, the persuasive power of the message, research shows, can be greatly diminished.

Research backs up this proposition. That is why, for example, advertisers often use doctors (or actors who play doctors on TV) to sell medicine or celebrities to tout fashion. However, the impact of source credibility can change over time. Hovland's research revealed that as time passes the receiver tends to forget the source but remember the message.

In the SVI campaign, many critics argued that the U.S. government was not a credible messenger. That's one of the reasons the SVI spots used real American Muslims and attributed CAMU as the sponsor of the ad.

Message Variables

What types of messages are most effective? Do rational appeals work more effectively than emotional appeals? What about the use of humor or fear in the message?

One of the most important variables that affects the persuasive power of a message is whether it presented a one-sided or two-sided view of a issue.

One-sided messages, those that only present arguments in favor of the desired change and ignore counter arguments, are most effective in persuading people who are already in favor of the message and those who are less educated. For an audience opposed to the message and/or a well-educated audience, a two-sided approach—one that presents both sides of the argument—tends to be more effective.

Presenting the arguments for and against the favored position allows the receivers to acknowledge their point of view before accepting the other side. Two-sided messages also serve to inoculate the audience against further efforts at persuasion.

In the case SVI—whose messages were one-sided—a two-sided message might have been more effective in persuading Arab and Muslim audiences in the short term. It also might have made them more resistant to anti-American messages in the future.

Receiver Variables

Most communicators claim that the first rule in effective communication is to know your audience. Receiver characteristics include demographic factors such as age, sex, income and education; personal factors such as personality, attitudes and beliefs; and social factors such as family, culture and social class.

When communicating with audiences in other countries, which is called cross-cultural communication, understanding the characteristics of the receiver can be difficult, but it is nonetheless important.

Hovland and other post-WWII researchers established the concept of individual differences and maintained that receivers have different fields of experience—backgrounds, personalities, values and environments. Individuals, therefore, will interpret and react differently to the same message.

Mass communication messages are not magic bullets that strike everyone in the same manner and result in an immediate, uniform, direct effect, as early propaganda scholars believed. Often effects are much more moderate and vary according to the characteristics of the individual receiver.

Hundreds of research studies have examined various receiver or audience characteristics. Hovland found that less educated people and those with lower self-esteem are easier to persuade than more educated and confident people.

Furthermore, attitude change may not happen quickly. Receivers who show no attitude change immediately following exposure to a persuasive message may show changes later—as late as six weeks after exposure. This phenomenon is called the "sleeper effect."

Two-Step Flow

Another important and well-established theory in mass communication is called two-step flow.[10] The basic idea is that the mass media do not influence everyone in society directly, but rather communication often flows through two steps—from the mass media to opinion leaders, who then pass messages on to others.

This concept is easily applied to advertising and consumer behavior. There are people in every community who are opinion leaders about certain subjects, such as the young man who knows all about music and stereos or the young woman who keeps up with the latest fashions. These individuals are also tuned to advertising messages about their favorite products, while many of the people they know may not pay attention to such ads.

However, when people need to buy a new CD player or party dress, they typically turn to a friend who is a recognized opinion leader about those products. The stereo fanatic and fashion maven are the opinion leaders for those items. They serve to inform their friends, family and colleagues about the latest products and best prices. Thus, the information flows in two steps, from the media to the opinion leader and then to others.

Media and Message Effectiveness

Even taking into account the theoretical underpinnings of persuasive communication, the question remains: How do advertisers determine if their messages work?

Within the advertising industry, there are widely accepted practical research techniques for measuring advertising effectiveness. One aspect of measurement, known as audience research, involves the advertisement's distribution. Another, called message research, deals with the message's effect on the audience. Did they see it? Did they understand it? Did they act on it?

Audience Research on SVI

Audience research, sometimes called media research, attempts to quantify the number of people exposed to a particular message.

Those who use U.S. audience research rely on companies such as Nielsen Media Research to provide estimates of the number of viewers of a program or the number of 'readers' of a newspaper or magazine carrying an ad. The ability of the media vehicle to attract an audience is known as reach, and the number of times the average viewer sees a particular ad is called frequency.

Media planners, those who specialize in message distribution strategies, select from multiple classes of media such as newspaper, magazines, television and Internet. They also choose vehicles within media—such as *The New York Times* or the CBS Evening

News—and timing patterns such as daily or weekly.

Media planners in the United States rely on measurement firms such as Nielsen to provide them with statistics regarding audience size and composition. These firms also provide data that allow media planners to target messages to specific audiences as defined by age, sex, geography, income and other variables.

SVI Media Plan

The media plan for SVI emphasized high reach, or coverage, by way of broad-brush carriers such as television and newspapers.

As is the case with many U.S. campaigns, radio—which is typically more geographically and demographically targeted than newspaper or television—was used as a support medium. Radio provided a way to 'fill in' the geographic holes not covered adequately by other media, and also provided additional frequency for the campaign.

Figure 5.2 is a slide from a McCann presentation to the State Department titled, "Media Framework," and dated October 28, 2002. It shows that the media strategy called for the SVI television spots to be 'set apart' from other commercial advertising, by running as stand-alone or solus spots, ideally to be positioned at the beginning of a commercial break.

It was hoped that SVI would be viewed almost as an extension of the programming rather than an advertisement. They nonetheless aired during normal commercial breaks and among commercials for other products and sponsors. In other words, they were treated like commercials.

The intensity, or weight, of a media schedule is calculated using gross rating points (GRPs). GRPs are simply the number of individuals exposed to the media vehicle carrying the ad expressed as a percentage of the total population. GRPs indicate audience accumulated each time the commercial airs or the newspaper ad runs. For example, if an ad in a particular newspaper reaches 10 percent of

Figure 5.2

Media Considerations

- Explore opportunities to position these mini-documentaries as programming and set them apart from mainstream commercial advertising despite airtime being paid for:
  - Solus (isolated) advertising slots
  - Sponsorship of relevant programming with social or political content which would allow placement of our vignettes as a part of the sponsorship presentation
  - First position in commercial breaks
  - Other local possibilities, e.g. dedicated programming time
- Local assessment on the possibility of roadblocks (airing the vignettes at the same time on multiple TV stations)
  - Start with the 120 sec versions of each mini-documentary over the initial two weeks to establish the messages. Then start to rotate 60 sec versions together with 120s with decreasing 120s vs 60s ratio towards the end of the campaign.
-

---

the target audience, it generates 10 GRPs. If the same ad runs five times, it will generate a total of 50 GRPs.

Table 5.1 depicts pre-launch predictions of GRP levels of the SVI campaign in seven countries where state-owned television advertising was sought. Table 5.2 indicates the projected GRP levels in countries slated to receive the spots via pan-Arab satellite over the five-week campaign.[11] The data show that SVI had an aggressive media schedule planned in terms of media weight or GRPs.

While audience measurement services such as Nielsen, Mediamark Research, Inc. and others provide fairly comprehensive estimates of U.S. audiences, sometimes such information is difficult to obtain in other countries.

For SVI, presumably accurate international television audience data were available to the McCann media planners. Based on McCann's memorandum to the State Department, the planned GRP

Table 5.1

Planned GRP, Reach and Frequency for SVI Campaign

Country	TV GRPs	Reach %	Average Frequency
Indonesia	1860	90%	21.3
Malaysia	1400	88%	15.9
Pakistan	1400	68%	20.6
Jordan	1795	65%	27.6
Lebanon	508	70%	7.3
Morocco	740	75%	10.0
Kuwait	907	55%	16.5

* Data taken from McCann-Erickson media documents as presented to the State Department.

**SVI television spots were scheduled but did not run in Jordan, Lebanon and Morocco.

levels were comparable to a fast-food or package goods campaign in the United States. Ample reach (up to 90% in Indonesia) and frequency (15 times on average) were delivered against the target markets.

Judging by the GRPs reported, it is evident that high coverage was achieved in the countries that agreed to run the SVI spots.

Table 5.2

GRPs levels via Pan-Arab Satellite

Country	TV GRPs
Saudi Arabia	589
Kuwait	618
United Arab Emirates	471
Bahrain	296
Oman	595
Qatar	423
Jordan	296

State Department documents offered one total audience estimate for the entire campaign at 288 million people as shown below:[12]

Indonesia	183.0 million
Pakistan	75.0 million
Pan-Arab	20.0 million
Malaysia	10.0 million
Kuwait	0.8 million

It should be noted that the media documents from the State Department were media plans—not final results. It is not certain whether the SVI ads actually ran at the intervals specified or with the frequency recommended. Advertisers typically order a post-buy analysis after a campaign runs to determine if the schedule was implemented as planned.

The internal State Department documents did not include such a post-buy report, and therefore information about the specific details of audiences delivered by the campaign is unknown. This is an important element in determining whether the SVI spots "worked" in specific countries. If the media plans did not run as scheduled, then the possibility exists that the messages were not seen often enough by an adequate number of people to be effective.

SVI Message Research

Message research describes what, if any, effect the message has on the intended audience. It answers basic questions such as, "Was the ad noticed or remembered?" as well as, "Was it liked?" and, of course, the ultimate question: "Does the ad make the consumer want to buy the product?"

It might seem that simply monitoring sales levels for a product during an ad campaign would be sufficient to determine if ads were working, but as will be discussed later in this chapter, advertising is only one of many factors related to consumer behavior.

In a document designed by 21 leading U.S. advertising agencies to outline best practice for copy testing—another term for message testing—Principle I reads as follows: "To be useful a copy test for a given advertisement should be designed to provide an assessment of the advertisement's potential for achieving its stated objectives ... any report on results should begin with a clear statement of the advertising objectives."[13]

Indeed, the debate about which advertising effects should be measured has a long history and remains an important topic in the industry today. Despite the prevalence of message testing activities in advertising, there is no general agreement that one single criterion is the most important to test.

Numerous message testing services are available, each with its own attendant theory or premise about how advertising works and how it should be evaluated. Most of the basic choices for measurement criteria are depicted in a variation of what is known as the Hierarchy of Effects model[14] (see Figure 5.2), so named because early in its history it was assumed that receivers of messages could "progress" through the hierarchy in relatively linear fashion. Knowledge, for instance, would precede the formulation of attitudes, and both would take place before a behavioral change resulted.

Later models took into account that consumers sometimes skip steps on the ladder of effects or do not navigate them in sequence. They could, for instance, move rather quickly from awareness to action in the case of an impulsive candy bar purchase, or more slowly for expensive or complex products such as cars or computers.

It is interesting to note here that most models of advertising culminate in a desired behavior or action on the part of the consumer—ultimately the purchase of a product or service—because most advertising is ultimately aimed at selling products. Yet the inability in most cases to assess the absolute contribution that a given ad campaign makes to sales of a product or service remains one of `the greatest sources of frustration for those in the advertising business.

Figure 5.2
Hierarchy of Effects Model

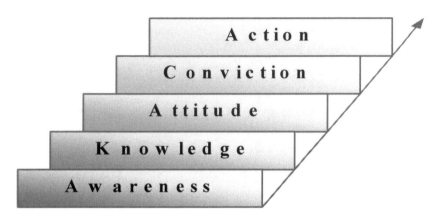

Having said that the purpose of most advertising is to sell products, determining specific return-on-investment (ROI) for each dollar of advertising expenditure continues to elude most advertisers—even the ones who spend tens of millions of dollars per year on television commercials.

Why is this so? The answer is that several factors—of which advertising is only one—contribute to whether a consumer will purchase a product or service or take some other action. Advertising is joined and sometimes upstaged by such forces as product pricing, advertising by competitive brands, weather conditions and word-of-mouth recommendations from friends or family. Isolating the degree to which advertising results in sales or other action is a very tricky process, and one too complicated to discuss in detail here.

Advertisers acknowledge the difficulty of linking advertising to specific sales levels or behavior. They believe, however, that lower level communication effects are often precursors to and set the stage for purchase. Therefore, measures of awareness, knowledge, attitude and conviction are often used to gauge advertising success, rather than behavioral measures alone.

In the case of SVI, determining whether the campaign worked must take into account that its primary objective was not to increase the sales of anything. The SVI spots were not tourism videos intended to promote travel to the United States, but rather to inform an audience about America and potentially affect attitudes. Though Beers consistently characterized the objective of SVI as opening a dialogue, which might imply a behavioral objective—two-way communication between the United States and the Muslim world—it is apparent that for the SVI television commercials the primary objective was simply to raise awareness about American values and religious tolerance. There was, in fact, one behavioral objective for the print elements of the campaign, though not for the television component. Print ads and the magazine *Muslim Life in America* contained direct-response opportunities.

Beers' team developed two paths for obtaining audience feedback: reader reply cards from the magazine *Muslim Life in America* and postings on the State Department Web site (www.opendialogue.com). Few of the findings from the feedback mechanisms were made public, other than brief mentions by Beers during interviews and in her testimony to Congress in February 2003.

An internal agency document indicated that the opendialogue.org Web site received more than one million hits. One State Department staffer who was immersed in the execution of the SVI campaign recalls seeing stacks of reply cards sitting on desks in State Department offices and reading numerous e-mails posted on opendialogue.org in response to the campaign, but doubted that responses were ever formally analyzed. Attempts to retrieve these SVI responses from the State Department were unsuccessful. Other than the personal recollection of Beers and her staff, the findings of these feedback mechanisms appear to be lost.

Given that SVI was a first-of-its-kind campaign and therefore no norms were in place with which its performance could be

Example page from opendialogue.org. The site is no longer active.

compared, it is difficult to judge whether one million Web site hits and thousands of reply cards constituted success from a behavioral standpoint. Nevertheless, the direct response figures appear to have been significant in terms of volume.

U.S. Favorability Polls

Well-publicized international public opinion polls taken periodically after 9/11 indicated an overall steady decline in U.S. favorability ratings.

If SVI was designed to improve attitudes toward the United States, then why did attitudes continue to deteriorate? The fact that polling figures did not reveal a completely consistent correlation between a country's exposure to SVI and subsequent improved attitudes toward the United States is perhaps the strongest argument that the campaign did not work. However, closer examination of the polling data reveals that this argument is not completely valid.

International polls conducted by various organizations showed mixed results—some countries exhibited more favorable attitudes toward the United States several months after the campaign, while others continued to decline. Using the Pew Global Attitudes Project[15] surveys as a guide, the following data emerge:

- In Indonesia, a country in which SVI ran, July 2002 (pre-SVI) U.S. favorability ratings were 61%, and then fell to 15% in May 2003.
- In Jordan, where the state-run television channel refused the SVI spots, favorability ratings dropped even more precipitously, from 25% in July 2002 to only 1% in May 2003.
- In Pakistan, where SVI ran in both print and broadcast, U.S. favorability scores rose from 10% to 13% during that same time.

Why didn't U.S. favorability ratings go up consistently in the countries where SVI aired? The answer to this question is confounded by the war in Iraq. The United States invaded Iraq in March 2003, which most likely explains the massive declines in favorability ratings in Indonesia and Jordan. The already low ratings in Pakistan may be a residual from the U.S. war in Afghanistan, which borders Pakistan.

The Pew surveys were not timed with SVI in mind. Rather, they ran on a schedule pre-determined by that organization and its field services, totally independent of the State Department and SVI planners.

Beyond the issue of timing is the issue of whether survey samples included individuals who had actually been exposed to SVI messages. The Pew studies were not set up to track SVI, and so information regarding whether a survey participant had seen the commercials was not captured. Had such information been collected, it would have been possible to compare, albeit six months after the campaign, responses from those who had seen it and those who had not.

Later in this chapter, specific information about a survey

measuring how well the SVI campaign was understood and remembered in Indonesia, conducted while the campaign was running, is presented. Chapter 6 will introduce additional studies on SVI effects that were conducted under laboratory conditions wherein it could be assured that participants were exposed to the SVI commercials, and that any change in attitude they exhibited before and after seeing the spots could be attributed to that exposure exclusively.

Timing of Message Research

There are four basic time categories related to message formulation and testing: developmental research, message pre-testing, message pilot-testing and message post-testing.

Developmental Message Research

This step precedes the creation of a message and is primarily concerned with determining which aspects of a product, service or idea are important to the consumer, as well as which strategic approach is most likely to succeed.

Research on consumer demographics, product preferences and motivation can be reviewed, and basic ideas for messages—variously referred to as appeals, concepts or promises—can be presented to consumers in focus groups or other settings to gauge interest.

A substantial amount of developmental research was conducted for the SVI campaign. Roper public opinion poll analyses detailed in Chapter 1 are examples of message development research involving quantitative studies in the target countries. Those surveys showed that, despite their differences on many issues and lifestyle factors, both Americans and people in predominantly Muslim countries considered the matters of faith, family and learning to be of great importance.

In terms of message approaches, agency personnel considered

at one point having non-Muslim Americans as spokespeople or co-spokespeople in the spots, but it was determined, presumably through research among the target audience, that a more powerful message would come from American Muslims exclusively.

Message Pre-Testing

The "pre" here refers to pre-campaign launch.

Pre-testing involves consumer evaluation of either rough or finished ads, and can be accomplished via focus groups, one-on-one interviews or Internet distribution of messages to consumer panels. Focus groups were conducted in Egypt, Indonesia and Turkey prior to the airing of the television spots.

Little specific information could be located on the extent of message pre-testing for SVI, but interviews with McCann-Erickson representatives revealed that in addition to the content changes made as the result of the legal clearance process, other edits and changes were made to rough versions of the commercials, based on focus group findings. One example was the deletion of part of a frame that featured a woman kneeling on rocks because it was feared that the image of such an act might be alienating to viewers who did not practice that custom.

Because embassy staffers were residents of the Muslim countries targeted, they were used as informal sounding boards for early versions of SVI messages. Beers noted that local customs prevented open interaction between men and women, making research interviews difficult to conduct.

Message Pilot-Testing

A pilot test usually calls for finished or almost-finished ads to be run in actual media on a small scale in order to assess how they are received in the marketplace. Sometimes this type of research is referred to as a test market, suggesting that reaction to a limited trial of a campaign might yield information that would lead to last-minute tweaks to increase effectiveness.

Although it is in theory highly desirable to have pilot-test feedback, in reality the practice is both time-consuming and expensive, and therefore is the most likely step in message testing to be skipped. As mentioned earlier, legal clearance issues resulted in the re-shooting and editing of the spots and a delay of several months that had already threatened the success of the campaign.

For these reasons a true pilot test was probably out of the question, but in retrospect many of the problems with the embassies and the press might have been anticipated and better inoculated against had a test market been employed.

Message Post-Testing

Conducted once a campaign is up and running, post-testing research can provide information about whether ads are noticed, if consumers registered an intended main message, and whether exposure resulted in changes in attitudes or intentions to act or buy.

In the case of informational campaigns such as SVI, post-testing can reveal whether an informational objective was met and whether the message was believable. Message post-testing is typically conducted via sample surveys of the target audience, using telephone, mail or Internet panel interviews.

SVI in Indonesia was evaluated using both surveys and personal interviews, including focus groups and person-on-the-street intercepts.

A large-scale telephone survey in Indonesia, conducted during the final weeks of the media schedule, was one such post-test undertaken for SVI.[16] Consumer research company NFO Worldwide used questions and methods of analysis similar to commercial brand research. Post-SVI tracking in Indonesia used measures of advertising awareness and main message learning or registration, as shown in Figures 5.3 and 5.4. By using the same measures employed by multinational brands, a direct comparison could be made between

Figure 5.3

A Framework for Interpretation: Awareness

Levels are at or above those of major consumer campaigns after four to six months of significantly higher spending.

	Prompted Recall	
Journalist Devianti	67%	⎤
Teacher Rawia Ismail	56%	⎬ During last 2 weeks
Baker Abdul-Raouf Hammuda	48%	⎦ of 5 week campaign
		Source: NFO Worldwide
Leading Soft Drink Campaign	36%	⎤ After 4 to 6 months
Leading Credit Card Campaign	54%	⎬ of heavy spending
Leading Computer Hardware Campaign	47%	⎦ Source: Audits and Surveys
United Way 2001Ad Awareness	62%	⎬ After 1 Year
Ad Council Colon Cancer Prevention	40%	⎦ Source: United Way & Ad Council

major U.S. ad campaigns and how SVI performed.

Figure 5.3 is part of a presentation taken from State Department documents and demonstrates that SVI enjoyed very healthy awareness and main message results. The "Journalist Devianti" spot about an Indonesian woman enrolled in the University of Missouri School of Journalism appeared to be the most memorable to the people of her own country, earning a 67% advertising recall score. This means that two-thirds of the sample questioned mentioned Devianti when the SVI spots were discussed.

McCann-Erickson attempted to put this figure into perspective with the use of various syndicated reports for some of the biggest advertising spenders for U.S. campaigns, which had netted recall scores from 36% to 54% after several months on air.

Likewise in Figure 5.4, with message recall—which goes beyond whether someone has remembered seeing a commercial to asking if they remembered any specific information from it—levels were also high, with 46% of Indonesian participants able to play back

Figure 5.4

A Framework for Interpretation

Message Playback levels after 3 weeks is comparable to those of major consumer brands after four to six month campaigns.

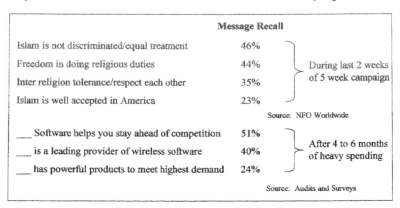

	Message Recall	
Islam is not discriminated/equal treatment	46%	
Freedom in doing religious duties	44%	During last 2 weeks of 5 week campaign
Inter religion tolerance/respect each other	35%	
Islam is well accepted in America	23%	
		Source: NFO Worldwide
___ Software helps you stay ahead of competition	51%	
___ is a leading provider of wireless software	40%	After 4 to 6 months of heavy spending
___ has powerful products to meet highest demand	24%	
		Source: Audits and Surveys

a main message that "Islam is not discriminated/equal treatment," "freedom in doing religious duties" (44%), or "inter-religion tolerance/respect each other" (35%).

The need to put such figures into perspective—aside from whether such cross-country comparisons were appropriate—is indicative of an apparent lack of appreciation on the part of those in public diplomacy for what an ad campaign is capable of achieving. The situation was complicated by the fact that Beers and advertising agency executives were forced to teach media and advertising basics while at the same time trying to demonstrate, using existing standards and norms, that their messages were working.

Two marketing communications researchers were contacted by the authors and asked if they would comment on media reach and post-testing tracking scores of "a hypothetical ad campaign run by Country A," which was trying to impart country-specific information about itself to citizens of "Country B."

In other words, advertising practitioners were asked to comment on the figures achieved by SVI, but without the attendant concern about politics and possibly their own cynicism about how futile it might be for the United States to affect hearts and minds in Muslim countries. They overwhelmingly endorsed the hypothetical numbers as successful, and added that spending levels must have been high to achieve such effects.

"[I]n my experience, these are numbers tough to get unless you a) are spending a bundle, b) spending it over a substantial period of time, and c) have pretty clear creative," said one former U.S. advertising agency account manager who is now a university professor. "Any consumer product would be thrilled if 50 percent-plus got the message with one campaign. Awareness is good, but changing attitudes is a whole lot harder. Any time an ad campaign can do that, I think it's a success."

The total amount spent on the SVI media buy—$5 million across five or more counties—is relatively low compared to most advertising campaigns. According to independent advertising experts, Beers' campaign got quite a "bang for the bucks."

According to an internal document that McCann-Erickson provided the State Department, both focus groups and one-on-one interviews were conducted in Jakarta during the SVI campaign. The document reports that focus group participants displayed "near universal awareness" of SVI.

> [M]ost participants viewed them positively and as an initiative to encourage dialogue between the U.S. and Indonesia. Participants expressed a desire to learn more about U.S. education and aid programs. Some commented that the documentaries had changed their perception about Muslims living in America. Some participants expressed skepticism regarding the campaign as 'propaganda,' but most gave credit for the intent behind it."

One-on-one person-on-the-street interviews in late November 2002 were compiled into a video presentation, according to the memo. "Here again, respondents were very much aware of the

Shared Values television and print campaign, and many reacted positively to the individual stories and the effort by the United States to speak directly to them."

Conclusion

So, did SVI work?

According to internal State Department documents about SVI in Indonesia, the campaign achieved its objectives. It not only got people talking about Muslim life in America, it also produced more positive perceptions of America.

An advertising tracking survey conducted around the third week of the five-week campaign yielded results for SVI on a par with or exceeding message play back for major U.S. advertisers that spend tens of millions of dollars communicating with American consumers.

Because the use of television spots to spread a U.S. message of religious tolerance abroad was new, there were no established public diplomacy advertising norms with which to compare its performance. Publication of tracking study statistics in this book constitutes the first chronicle of such quantitative performance scores and provides some indication of what to expect in future research.

Taken together, the audience research and tracking research indicate that SVI appeared successful in view of stated campaign goals among its target audiences—a finding that stands in stark contrast to the very negative reviews the effort received from politicians, media critics and others.

This chapter was concerned primarily with media delivery and message registration of the SVI spots. Many would argue, however, that seeing and understanding a message does not equate with changing deeply held attitudes. The next chapter will explore other measures of campaign effectiveness, including attitude change.

Chapter Endnotes

[1]Atika Schubert, "U.S. tests charm offensive in Indonesia," CNN.com, 31 October 2002. Retrieved from http://edition.cnn.com/2002/WORLD/asiapcf/southeast/10/31/indonesia.us.campaign/ on 4 November 2005.

[2]Ibid. An Indonesian homemaker said, "I think it's effective enough. This way we can get to know Muslims in the U.S. that are not discriminated against. It seems that those who are suspected as terrorists, if we didn't know better, are all Muslims. Muslims are accused as terrorists. I think this ad is good because it addresses that." A kebab stall owner said his favorite video was a story about a Lebanese baker in Ohio—a shop owner like himself, struggling to raise a modern Muslim family. "I like this one the best, because it's about togetherness. You can see the family praying and they show they can pray anywhere. It shows that we are the same."

[3]Anonymous former State Department staffer, interview by authors, 12 August 2005, San Antonio, TX.

[4]William F. Arens, *Contemporary Advertising,* 6th ed., (Chicago: Irwin, 1996), p. 6.

[5]This model is based on the work of Wilbur Schramm. For a complete discussion of the communication process, see Wilbur Schramm, "The Nature of Communication Between Humans," in *The Process and Effects of Mass Communication,* ed. Wilbur Schramm and Donald F. Roberts (Urbana, IL: University of Illinois Press, 1977), pp. 3-53.

[6]James M. Olson and Mark P. Zanna, "Attitudes and attitude change," *Annual Review of Psychology,* 44 (1993), p. 135.

[7]For a full discussion of persuasion and the history of persuasion see Anthony Pratkanis and Elliot Aronson, *Age of Propaganda: The Everyday Use and Abuse of Persuasion,* rev. ed. (New York: Owl Book, 2001).

[8]The "Smokey the bear/Only you can prevent forest fires" campaign began in 1944 and remains the longest running public service announcement ever produced by the American Ad Council. For more information see http://www.smokeybear.com/vault/default.asp.

[9]For a full discussion of Hovland's persuasion research see Shearon Lowery and Melvin DeFleur, *Milestones in Mass Communication Research: Media Effects,* 3rd ed. (White Plains, NY: Longman, 1995), pp. 165-188.

[10]Two-step flow was first hypothesized in the Erie County election studies, see Paul F. Lazarsfeld, Bernard Berelson, and Hazel Gaudet, *The People's Choice* (New York: Columbia University Press, 1948). Also see Elihu Katz, "The two-step flow of communication: An up-to-date report of an hypothesis," *Public Opinion Quarterly,* Vol. 21 (1957), pp. 61-78.

[11]Projected GRP levels were obtained from internal documents that were produced by McCann-Erickson advertising agency for Beers' team in October 2002.

[12]Penetration statistics for SVI obtained from email message from McCann staffers to Beers' team dated 19 December 2002.

[13]Advertising Research Foundation, "Positioning of Advertising Copy Testing statement," 1982.

[14]Robert J. Lavidge and Gary A. Steiner, "A Model for Predictive Measurement of Advertising Effectiveness," *Journal of Marketing,* 25, (October, 1961).

[15] Pew Research Center for the People and the Press, *What the World Thinks in 2002: How Global Publics View Their Lives, Their Countries, the World, America.* (Washington, DC: The Pew Research Center, December 2002). Retrieved from http://people-press.org/reports/pdf/165.pdf on March 22, 2004; Pew Research Center for the People and the Press, *A Year After Iraq War: Mistrust of America in Europe Ever Higher, Muslim Anger Persists,* (Washington, DC: The Pew Research Center, March 2004). Retrieved on March 22 2004, from http://people-press.org/reports/pdf/206.pdf. Also see United States General Accounting Office, "State Department and the Broadcasting Board of Governors expand efforts in the Middle East but face significant challenges," *GAO Highlights GAO-04-435T, Testimony before the Subcommittee on National Security, Emerging Threats, and International Relations,* 10 February 2004.

[16]Findings of post-campaign survey in Indonesia were obtained from internal memorandum from McCann advertising to Beers dated 11 February 2003. Beers discussed the findings publicly in a Senate Committee on Foreign Relations hearing on American Public Diplomacy and Islam, 27 February 2003. Retrieved from foreign.senate.gov/testimony/2003/ BeersTestimony030227.pdf on 5 November 2005.

Chapter 6

Did Shared Values Work? Results of Experiments and Diagnostic Copy Tests

The Shared Values Initiative campaign was effective, not only in starting a dialogue with the Muslim world, which was Charlotte Beers' goal, but also in changing attitudes toward America, according to experimental research and diagnostic copy tests. In this chapter, we present the results of our own quasi-experimental research, which involved showing the advertisements to more than 500 students from more than three dozen different countries.

Although the main goal of the Shared Values Initiative (SVI) campaign, according to Charlotte Beers, was to "start a dialogue" between people in the Middle East and America, most critics focused instead on whether the campaign was successful in changing attitudes toward America. This focus is not surprising, given the deterioration of America's image after 9/11 and the expectation that public diplomacy programs would "win the hearts and minds" of people in the Middle East and elsewhere.

The SVI campaign was clearly successful in generating high recall scores in Indonesia, as Chapter 5 pointed out. But tracking studies did not focus on whether the advertisements changed overall attitudes toward the United States. Were viewers more likely after seeing the commercials to perceive the United States as being tolerant of Muslims and the Islamic faith? Did their views toward America become more favorable?

To answer these questions, we conducted pre-post experiments and diagnostic copy tests in three countries. The data were collected from more than 500 international students from 39 countries.[1]

Laboratory versus Field Research

The data reported in Chapter 5 were examples of field research. They were collected in Indonesia among populations who had seen the SVI commercials under normal viewing conditions.

One of the advantages of such studies is that they are conducted in the so-called real world and, thus, can be generalized to the entire population when probability sampling methods are employed. However, one of the disadvantages of field research is that it is difficult to make conclusions about cause and effect.

For that, the laboratory experiment is more appropriate, where confounding effects or factors can be more highly controlled. The purpose of our experiments was not to establish who had seen the commercials, as that had already been done in Indonesia with the post-campaign surveys and with estimates of audience size in other countries. Rather, the experiments were designed to assess whether the SVI commercials could change attitudes toward the United States and identify how those attitudes change.

Samples

More than 500 non-American college students from around the world participated in the experiments, which were conducted from July 2003 to September 2005 in London, Singapore and Cairo.

Our home universities paid for the research in the first two countries.[2] Oklahoma State University doctoral candidate Matt

Hamilton gathered the data in Singapore as part of his dissertation. Professor Kevin Keenan administered the study for us in Cairo.

London Sample 1

We conducted two separate studies in London. The first sample included 105 international students taking courses at Regents College in July 2003. Fifty-four percent were female and 46% were male. The youngest was 16 and the oldest was 41. The average was 22.

More than half (58%) spoke English fluently, and all were studying in English. The 105 students were from 25 different countries, with European countries accounting for nearly 70% and the remainder coming from the Middle East/India (10.5%), East Asia (9.5%); Africa (5.7%) and South America (3.8%).

More than half of participants were Christian (57.1%), 5.8% were Muslim, 12.4% checked "other" as a religious option, 20% said they were "not religious," and five respondents refused to answer. Forty-one percent said they had visited the United States.

London Sample 2

We went back to London in May 2004 to replicate the study, which included an additional 47 international students who also were taking courses at Regents College.

We did this partly to increase the sample sizes, especially for Muslims, who were a primary target market for the commercials. When the findings of the first London study were published online and in the *Journal of Advertising Research*,[3] critics were quick to dismiss the data because the number of Muslims in the sample was small.[4] We eventually were able to boost the total number of Muslims to 87.

Thirty-six percent of students in the second London study were female and 64% were male. Their average age was 22 with a range of 17 to 40.

English was spoken fluently by 91%, and all were studying in

English. The 47 students represented 23 different countries, with European countries (including Russia) accounting for 58%; 15.5% from the Middle East/India; 6.6% from Africa; 11% from Mexico/Canada; and 8.8% from South America.

Nearly half of participants were Christian (44.7%), 17% were Muslim, 11% were Hindu, 7% were Jewish, 9% checked "other" as a religious option, 9% said they were "not religious," and two respondents refused to answer. Sixty-eight percent said they had visited the United States.

Because of the relatively small sample size for this study, only data for the experiment are presented. Subgroup analyses and data for the copy test are excluded, but the findings for this sample were nearly identical to those for the first London study.

Singapore Sample

A total of 328 students in advanced diploma and bachelor's degree programs at the Management Development Institute participated in the study, which was conducted in Singapore in March 2004.

Seventy percent of the students were female, and 30% were male. Average age of the participants was 24, with a range of 16 to 43. Ninety-five percent said they spoke English fluently. One-third (35.4%) had visited the United States, and 95.8% said they would like to do so.

Most participants were Singaporean (86.7%), followed by Chinese (6.0%), and Malaysian (4.1%). In terms of ethnicity, the majority of students were Chinese (70.9%), followed by Indian (11.5%), Malaysian (10.5%), Eurasian (2.0%) and Japanese (1.4%).

The largest group of students that expressed a religious preference was Christian (36.2%), followed by Buddhist (17.6%), Muslim (13.0%), Taoist (3.4%), Hindu (3.0%) and Jewish (0.3%). Other responses were "not religious" (13.9%), "other" (5.3%), and 3.1 percent refused to answer.

Cairo Sample

In summer 2005, Professor Kevin Keenan replicated the experiment at the American University in Cairo, Egypt. We asked him to do this partly to see whether the findings would hold up in a Muslim country and partly to increase the number of Muslim students in our sample for subgroup comparisons.

The Egyptian sample included 38 undergraduate students in advertising and marketing. Eighty percent were female and 20 percent were male. They ranged in age from 19 to 43 and the average age was 24.

Ninety-five percent spoke English fluently. About half (47.2%) had visited the United States. The largest group that expressed a religious preference was Muslim (n=31). Four were Christian and three refused to indicate their religion.

Because of the small sample size, only the findings for the experiment are presented.

Research Design

A quasi-experimental method was employed. All of the students viewed the SVI commercials and completed questionnaires before and after viewing the commercials.

We chose not to employ a control group because of limited resources. We felt it was more important to have a larger sample and that the results of a control group would not differ significantly from those of the pre-viewing. Since no other stimulus was introduced into the participants' environment, and since the time period between measures was only 10 minutes, we do not believe the decision not to use a control group compromised the study.

Students who participated in the experiments first completed a written questionnaire regarding their attitudes toward the U.S. government, the U.S. people and whether Muslims were treated fairly

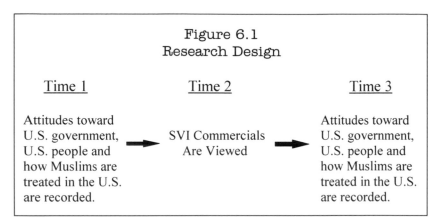

Figure 6.1
Research Design

Time 1	Time 2	Time 3
Attitudes toward U.S. government, U.S. people and how Muslims are treated in the U.S. are recorded.	SVI Commercials Are Viewed	Attitudes toward U.S. government, U.S. people and how Muslims are treated in the U.S. are recorded.

in America. They were then shown the SVI commercials, after which they completed a post-test questionnaire containing the same attitudinal questions (see Figure 6.1). The three questions were:

- Please tell us if you have a very favorable (4), somewhat favorable (3), somewhat unfavorable (2) or very unfavorable (1) opinion of the government of the United States?
- Please tell us if you have a very favorable (4), somewhat favorable (3), somewhat unfavorable (2) or very unfavorable (1) opinion of the U.S. people?
- How strongly do you agree or disagree with the following statement? Muslims who live in America are treated fairly. (Responses: 5=strongly agree; 4=agree; 3=neither agree nor disagree; 2=disagree; 1=strongly disagree)

Findings: Attitude Change

In general, the findings show that viewing the commercials improved students' attitudes toward the United States, especially in terms of perceptions of how Muslims are treated. Moreover, the findings show that the effects were somewhat stronger for Muslim students than for Christians and others.

Attitude Toward U.S. Government

In three of the four samples, attitude toward the U.S. government was more positive after viewing the SVI commercials.

Table 6.1 shows that students in the first London sample gave the U.S. government a mean rating of 1.86 in the pretest, compared with 2.05 in the post-test. In the second London sample, the ratings were 1.68 and 1.95. Students in the Singapore sample held more positive attitudes than students in both of the London studies (2.42 vs. 1.86 and 1.68, respectively), and their mean attitude score also was higher (2.65) after viewing the SVI commercials. All of these differences are statistically significant at a 95 percent level of confidence ($p<.05$), which means they likely did not occur by chance but, rather, can be attributed to the experimental stimulus (i.e., viewing the SVI spots).

In Cairo, the mean value on this measure also increased after viewing the commercials, but the increase is not statistically significant. Because of the small sample size there, a relatively high degree of difference is necessary to obtain statistical significance.

Attitude Toward U.S. People

Unlike the findings for attitude toward the U.S. government, in three of the four samples, attitude toward the U.S. people did not change significantly after viewing the commercials. In both of the London samples and the Cairo sample, viewing the commercials did not change the students' attitudes toward U.S. people. However, the ratings on this measure did increase somewhat in Singapore.

Table 6.1 shows that before viewing the commercials, students in first London sample gave the American people a mean rating of 2.74, compared with 2.84 in the post-test. The ratings in the second sample were 2.80 vs. 2.88. The mean values in Cairo were 3.09 and 3.06. None of these changes is statistically significant.

However, students in the Singapore sample gave the American

Advertising's War on Terrorism

Table 6.1
Effect of Commercials on Attitudes

Attitude/Sample	Mean score before viewing SVI commercials	Mean score after viewing SVI commercials
Opinion toward U.S. Government**		
London Sample 1 (N=105)	1.86	2.05*
London Sample 2 (N=47)	1.68	1.95*
Singapore Sample (N=328)	2.42	2.65*
Cairo Sample (N=38)	1.55	1.76
Opinion toward U.S. people**		
London Sample 1 (N= 105)	2.74	2.84
London Sample 2 (N=47)	2.80	2.88
Singapore Sample (N=328)	2.84	2.91*
Cairo Sample (N=38)	3.09	3.06
Treatment of Muslims***		
London Sample 1 (N=105)	2.82	3.14*
London Sample 2 (N=47)	2.80	3.24*
Singapore Sample (N=328)	2.81	3.20*
Cairo Sample (N=38)	2.53	2.92*

*Results are statistically significant at the 95 percent level of confidence ($p<.05$).
**Four-point rating scale
***Five-point rating scale

people a slightly higher rating after viewing the commercials (2.84 vs. 2.91; $p<.05$).

Attitudes Toward Treatment of Muslims

In all four studies, attitude scores toward the treatment of Muslims in America improved significantly after viewing the commercials. The changes on this measure also were greater than those for the first measures (attitude toward the U.S.).

Table 6.1 shows that before viewing the commercials, students in the first London sample gave the United States a 2.82 mean rating (five-point scale) in terms of how it treats Muslims, compared with 3.14 for the post-test. The ratings for students in the second London sample were 2.80 and 3.24. In Singapore, the ratings went from 2.81 to 3.20. And in Cairo, which had the smallest sample, the ratings went from 2.53 to 2.92. All of these changes were statistically significant.

The fact that the commercials had more impact on this measure is not surprising, because the main message in the commercials was focused on the treatment of Muslims in America and not on general attitudes toward the U.S. government and U.S. people.

Findings: Demographic Differences

In general, the commercials had a greater, more "positive" effect on Muslims than on Christians and other groups. Gender and location also had some effect on the results.

Muslim Students vs. Others

The most striking—and perhaps surprising—finding is that Muslims reacted more favorably to the SVI commercials than Christians and other groups. This was even true in Cairo.

The change was most pronounced on the attitude about how Muslims are treated in the United States. This was the case even though Muslims were initially more critical of the United States. Table 6.2 shows that in the pretest, Muslim students in all four samples gave lower ratings on this measure than Christian students.

But this initial skepticism apparently did not innoculate the Muslim students from the effects of the commercials. In fact, Table 6.2 shows that in three of the four studies, the mean scores that Muslims students gave on this measure increased significantly after

Table 6.2
Effect of Religious Affiliation on Attitude about
How Muslims Are Treated in the United States

Sample/Religious Affiliation	Mean score before viewing SVI commercials	Mean score after viewing SVI commercials
London Sample 1		
Muslims (N=6)	2.83	3.33
Christians (N=60)	2.95	3.22*
All Others (N=34)	2.65	3.06*
London Sample 2		
Muslims (N=8)	2.25	3.25*
Christians (N=21)	2.90	2.95
All Others (N=16)	3.00	3.56*
Singapore Sample		
Muslims (N=42)	2.71	3.26*
Christians (N=119)	2.79	3.11*
All Others (N=137)	2.85	3.27*
Cairo Sample		
Muslims (N=31)	2.32	2.77*
Christians (N=4)	4.00	4.00

*Results are statistically significant at the 95 percent level of confidence ($p<.05$). Caution should be used in interpreting the significance findings for Muslims in the London Sample 2 because of the small sample size. Data excludes respondents who refused to answer the religious affiliation question.

viewing the commercials. This includes the London sample 2, which only included 8 Muslim students. The results for the first London sample, which only included 6 Muslim students, were not statistically significant.

These findings also generally applied to the other two measures (attitude toward the U.S. government and attitude toward the U.S. people), although the effects were less pronounced because the content of the commercials focused more on how Muslims are treated than on general perceptions of the United States (data not shown).

In the first London sample, the commercials did not significantly alter the attitudes of Christians and "not religious" respondents. But Muslims and "others" showed positive shifts in attitudes toward the U.S. government post viewing (data not shown). In the Singaporean study, Malays, who are primarily Muslim, exhibited the most positive attitudes toward the U.S. people after seeing the commercials, and they also had the most positive attitude and posted the largest increase in score regarding how Muslims in the United States are treated.

Muslims in the Singapore study held the most positive attitudes toward the U.S. people after seeing the SVI commercials. Singaporeans who had never visited the United States also had significantly more positive attitudes about how fairly Muslims are treated in America after exposure to the SVI messages.

Malay Muslim women who had not visited the United States were most strongly affected by the commercials. After viewing the commercials, the mean scores on all three measures for these women were much higher than their male counterparts.

Other Demographics

Prior to viewing the spots, women in the London study had a more favorable attitude toward the United States people than men (data not shown).

There also were significant differences in attitude toward the U.S. people both before and after viewing the videos among different geographic groups, with European students holding less favorable attitudes toward the people of the United States than students from other parts of the world. This difference may stem from increased economic and political competition between the United States and

Europe since the end of the Cold War and from negative reactions to the U.S.-led war in Iraq.

Diagnostic Copy Tests

While experiments are conducted to study cause-and-effect relationships, copy tests are used to study consumer reaction to the ad itself. Copy tests focus attention on the content and, thus, seek to learn more about the effectiveness of the advertisements. Advertisers use copy tests to obtain feedback on the creative elements of a message: Did the audience get the intended message? Was the message believable? Did they like the message?

A post-campaign survey, such as the SVI Indonesia study detailed in Chapter 5, is one form of a copy test. It is conducted once a campaign has run. The results of that SVI tracking study, which were completed via telephone after the third week of the television schedule, revealed strong recall scores for the SVI spots—up to 67% for individual commercials. Almost half of those interviewed correctly played back the intended main message that Muslims enjoy religious freedom in the United States.

We administered a copy test on the students who participated in the London and Singapore experiments. Our test sought to answer the following question: "Why did the students react to the commercials the way they did?"

The copy test we used was similar to those used in the advertising industry.[5] Such studies typically include both closed-ended items (dichotomous "yes/no" questions and multiple-response categories) and open-ended questions, which allow respondents to answer in their own words.

The closed-ended items included:

- believability of commercials to self and others (5-point scale)
- effectiveness of commercials (5-point scale)

- appropriateness of commercials (5-point scale)
- presence of confusing elements (dichotomous, then open-ended)

The open-ended items included:

- first impression of commercials
- main message, and
- aspects liked most/least about commercials

First Impressions

After viewing the commercials, students were asked, "What was the first thing that came to your mind when you viewed these video segments?"

More than half of the students had positive or neutral comments about the commercials. These are grouped under three headings in Table 6.3: "Image of the United States," "Muslim Life in the United States," and "Positive Reactions (nonspecific)." More than a fourth of the London students (28.6%) and more than one out of seven Singaporean students (14.9%) mentioned "Image," which included comments such as "positive image of the United States," "acceptance/respect for other cultures," "opportunities/freedom," and "efforts to improve image after 9/11."

About a fourth in each group (23.8% London and 26.8% Singapore) mentioned "Muslim Life," which included "how Muslims live in the United States," "Muslims are respected/accepted/free in America," and "Muslim life after 9/11." Fewer than one in 10 mentioned other nonspecific positive elements.

Although more than half of the students had positive or neutral comments to say about the commercials, many of the respondents in London and Singapore also had negative first impressions to the commercials (44.8% and 41.8%, respectively). Most of those impressions challenged the veracity of the commercials and included comments like "not true," "fake," "suspicious," "propaganda,"

Table 6.3
First Impression of Shared Values Commercials

	London Sample (N=105)		Singapore Sample (N=328)	
	N	%	N	%
<u>Negative Reactions (non-specific)</u>	<u>47</u>	<u>44.8</u>	<u>137</u>	<u>41.8</u>
Not true/fake/suspicious/could backfire/ staged	19		19	
Propaganda/public relations/ persuasion	13		72	
Misleading/one-sided	7		18	
Skeptical/unsure/hopeful/curious	6		15	
Why were the videos made?	2		7	
Racism	0		3	
Iraq War	0		2	
Waste of time	0		1	
<u>Image of the United States</u>	<u>30</u>	<u>28.6</u>	<u>49</u>	<u>14.9</u>
Positive image of United States/"best behavior"	7		4	
Acceptance/respect for other cultures	6		0	
Opportunities/freedom	5		6	
Americans like/accept Muslims	4		0	
Kind/"Beautiful" people/caring	2		1	
Efforts to improve image after 9/11	2		11	
Other image	2		0	
American people vs. government	1		0	
Americans justifying "actions"	1		0	
<u>Muslim Life in the United States</u>	<u>25</u>	<u>23.8</u>	<u>88</u>	<u>26.8</u>
How Muslims live in the United States	7		33	
Muslims are respected/accepted/free in America	6		28	
Muslim life after 9/11	6		10	
Muslims like the United States	3		2	
Muslims can practice religion freely	2		7	
Happy Muslims in the United States	1		7	
Muslims have social values	0		1	
<u>Positive Reactions (nonspecific)</u>	<u>9</u>	<u>8.6</u>	<u>23</u>	<u>7.0</u>
Friendly/good/cool/awesome/interesting	8		10	
Appropriate for situation	1		10	
Promote Peace	0		3	
Other	7	6.7	31	9.5

Question: What was the first thing that came to your mind when you viewed these video segments?

"public relations," "misleading" and "one-sided." Half of the Singaporean students with initial negative reactions (72 of 137) used the terms "propaganda" or "public relations campaign" in their responses, possibly because of the Singapore government's use of propaganda campaigns about the country's social issues.[6] Samples of the verbatim responses to the first impression question are available in Table 6.4.

Main Message

Students also were asked to identify "the main message that these video segments are trying to communicate" to them.

The vast majority were able to identify some of the main themes that Charlotte Beers sought in the commercials. Table 6.5 shows that the most frequent response in the London sample dealt with "Image of the United States." More than 6 of 10 students (61%) mentioned "Image," which included comments like "acceptance/respect of other cultures and religions," "opportunities/freedom," and "Americans like/accept Muslims."

Students from Singapore were less likely to mention "Image" (39.3%), but they were more likely than the London students to mention something pertaining to "Muslim Life in the United States" (53.0% vs. 32.4%). The most frequent response was "Muslims are treated equally/accepted/free in America." More than a third of the entire sample mentioned that. These playback scores are high and are comparable to successful commercial advertising campaigns in the United States. Samples of the verbatim comments are available in Table 6.6.

Believability of Commercials

Although many of the students had positive first impressions of the commercials and understood the message embedded within them, did they believe what they saw? The answer is mixed.

About half of the students in all three samples said the SVI

Table 6.4
Sample Verbatims of First Impressions

Negative Reactions:

Rather unbelievable as there had been so many news and reports of war waged between Muslims and the Americans, eg. George Bush and Osama bin Laden. Student from Singapore study.

Propaganda. Selective advertising. False representation! Student from Singapore study.

Rubbish. Advertising is a deceptive persuader. The advertisements show Muslims who have been corrupted by the U.S. to say good things. How about those Muslims who do not have as many pleasant experiences? Why don't I see their views? Student from Singapore study.

All countries attempt to promote their policies—some fail. Some succeed. Good luck! But actions speak louder than words. Student from London study.

It seems to show just positive aspects for foreigners living in the U.S. Student from London study.

Image of the United States:

That it's a good thing for a Muslim to be living there. As a Muslim myself, I didn't think that Muslims can really survive in the U.S. Student from Singapore study.

Muslims living in the United States still stay rooted to their faith and values, despite living in another country and the freedom given to them contributes to this situation. Student from Singapore study.

It was an advertisement about American freedom. Student from London study.

The U.S. government tried to give a good image in the Muslims world. By exaggerating and modifying the truth. That is 100% propaganda. Student from London study.

Muslim Life in the United States:

How Muslims live in USA, they are living peacefully with all other religious people. Student from Singapore study.

Muslims are welcome in the United States. Student from Singapore study.

How Muslims adapt themselves—They behave like they're at "home." Student from London study.

It is interesting/good to see how Muslims live in the USA. Student from London study.

Positive Reactions:

Great! They want the U.S. people to know about the Muslim people, their life, family, etc. Student from Singapore Study.

Good advertisement. I felt like there was a need to demonstrate that USA is accepting Muslims. Student from London study.

I really found this video interesting b/c it has given me the idea of American society (or a part of it). Student from London study.

Table 6.5
Main Message of Shared Values Commercials

	London Sample (N=105)		Singapore Sample (N=328)	
	N	%	N	%
Image of the United States	64	61.0	129	39.3
Image of United States/"best behavior"	7		0	
Acceptance/respect for other cultures/religions	22		79	
Opportunities/freedom	11		7	
Americans like/accept Muslims	16		0	
Efforts to improve image after 9/11	3		18	
Other image	2		0	
Americans are not fighting against Muslims	2		2	
American people vs. government	1		1	
Americans are fair/caring/friendly	0		9	
Positive image of the United States	0		8	
Trying to restore ties with Muslims	0		5	
Muslim Life in the United States	34	32.4	174	53.0
How Muslims live in the United States	12		22	
Muslims are respected/accepted/free in America	11		135	
Muslims can practice religion freely	6		7	
Happy Muslims in the United States	5		10	
Negative Reactions (non-specific)	5	4.8	5	1.5
Not true/fake/suspicious/could backfire/	2		2	
Misleading/one-sided	1		0	
Skeptical/unsure/hopeful	2		1	
Condescending	0		2	
Other	4	3.8	20	6.1
People can live together	1		0	
Don't know/no comment	1		2	
Miscellaneous	2		0	
All Muslims are not terrorists/bad people	0		11	
Blank (no answer)	0		6	
Entertaining	0		1	

Question: In your own words, what is the main message that these video segments are trying to communicate to you?

commercials were "very" or "somewhat" believable or credible to them (see Table 6.7). Students in Singapore were somewhat more likely than those in both of the London samples to say this (61.6% vs. 47.1% and 52.3%, respectively).

Table 6.6
Sample Verbatims of Main Message

Image of the United States:

  That America is not prejudiced against members of other ethnic groups or other religions. Student from Singapore study.

  America embraces every race/religion including Muslims. Student from Singapore study.

  After 9/11, Americans do not discriminate against the Muslims living in U.S. but instead they were given an opportunity to perform their job. Student from the Singapore study.

  They are trying to show that the U.S. is the country of freedom and fairness. Student from London study.

  We are for freedom; therefore, we accept all the people. Student from London study.

Muslim Life in the United States:

  That Muslims are treated justly and fairly in America. Student from Singapore study.

  That America welcomes Muslims and respect them despite all that they are trying to do to eliminate Muslim terrorists/extremists. Student from Singapore study.

  Muslims have equal privilege and opportunities, doesn't face prejudice or discriminations and can practice their religion effectively. Student from Singapore study.

  Save the politics for the extremist groups. Americans and Muslims are suitable to live together. Student from London study.

  The video wants to communicate that the Muslims are happy to live in America. Student from London study.

Negative Reactions:

  That if the U.S. could come up with something like this they must be really desperate. Student from Singapore study.

  I don't know American people like that. Student from London study.

  It might not be that American people are good & understanding with other religions, they love Muslims! (but it is not the case). Student from London study.

All three groups were less likely to say the commercials would be "believable or credible ... to their intended audiences in other countries" (35.1% for the first London sample, 46.7% for the second, and 43.6% for Singapore). Analysis of written comments suggests that their major concern was the one-sided and overly positive tone

Table 6.7
Believability, Appropriateness and
Perceived Effectiveness of the Commercials

	Top Two Box Score %	Mean Rating
Believability to Self (4-point scale)*		
London Sample 1 (N=105)	47.1	2.30
London Sample 2 (N=47)	52.3	2.43
Singapore Sample (N=328)	61.6	2.62
Believability to Others (4-point scale)*		
London Sample 1 (N= 105)	35.1	2.15
London Sample 2 (N=47)	46.7	2.29
Singapore Sample (N=328)	43.6	2.41
Appropriateness (5-point scale)**		
London Sample 1 (N= 105)	38.1	2.93
London Sample 2 (N=47)	47.8	3.11
Singapore Sample (N=328)	52.4	3.40
Effectiveness (5-point scale)**		
London Sample 1 (N=105)	46.6	3.15
London Sample 2 (N=47)	44.6	3.25
Singapore Sample (N=328)	52.1	3.40

Top 2 box is the sum of those who answered the most positive response (such as "strongly agree") and the second most positive response (such as "somewhat agree").

*The believability questions were worded as follows: (a.) "How believable or credible are the videos to YOU?" (b) "How believable or credible do you think the videos will be to their intended audiences in other countries?" Responses were recorded on a 4-point scale: 4=very believable, 3=somewhat believable, 2=somewhat unbelievable, 1=very unbelievable.

**The appropriateness and effectiveness statements were worded as follows: (a) "I think it is appropriate and helpful for the U.S. government to run these commercials on television stations in other countries, including Muslim countries." (b) "I think the videos are an effective tool in communicating with citizens of Muslim countries about the positive aspects of American life." Responses were recorded on a 5-point scale: 5=strongly agree, 4=agree, 3=neither agree nor disagree, 2=disagree, 1=strongly disagree.

of the spots. Many said they did not believe the factual content or found them unrealistically positive in light of news coverage of events involving mistreatment of American Muslims.

Among geographic subgroups in the London study, Europeans judged the spots as significantly less believable compared with participants from other countries. Likewise, among religious subgroups, Christians and those "not religious" judged the commercials to be less believable than other religious groups, including Muslims.

Appropriateness of Commercials

The students also were divided on the issue of whether "it is appropriate and helpful for the U.S. Government to run these commercials on television stations in other countries, including Muslim countries." Table 6.7 shows that nearly 4 of 10 students in the first London sample (38.1%), nearly 5 of 10 in the second sample (47.8%) and more than half of the Singaporean students (52.4%) said it was appropriate.

Subgroup analysis of the London study showed that Europeans considered it less appropriate and helpful for the United States to air the spots compared with students from other geographic regions. Muslims were more positive than other religious groups about the use of the SVI spots in Muslim countries. Overall, Muslim students were more favorable toward the SVI campaign than were other groups.

Effectiveness of the Commercials

Students were also divided on whether they thought the "videos are an effective tool in communicating with citizens of Muslim countries about the positive aspects of American life." Figure 6.7 shows that more than half (52.1%) of the Singaporean students and nearly half of the London students (46.6% in sample one and 44.6% in sample two) agreed that the ads were an effective tool.

Subgroup analysis of London participants showed that women

agreed more strongly than men that the spots were an effective tool. Additionally, those who had visited the United States, as well as those who were fluent in English, were less likely to agree the spots were effective.

Elements Liked and Disliked

Students were asked what they liked and disliked about the SVI commercials.

Although nearly a fourth of those who rated the spots said there was "nothing" they liked about them, three-fourths mentioned something they liked (see Table 6.8). The most frequent responses were categorized as dealing with the "tone/point of view/style." More specifically, about a third of the students in both samples said the videos were "friendly/happy/positive/uplifting," "normal people/ diverse, different people," or "objective/realistic."

The rest of the responses were divided among three major categories: "Overall Concept and Information Content," "Information about Muslims," and "Information about the United States." Samples of the verbatims are contained in Table 6.9.

By far the most disliked aspect of the videos was their lack of believability (see Table 6.10). About two-thirds of the London students (67.5%) and one-third of the Singapore students (33.0%) said the commercials were misleading, false, not real, one-sided, biased, too good to be true, or too positive.

Consistent with previous findings, the London sample was more critical of the content. The Singapore students, in contrast, were more likely to say there was nothing they disliked about the content (24.4% vs. 8.6%). Only a small number of students mentioned that they did not like specific executional elements, such as the "from the American people" ending or the fact that only Muslims were featured. Some in the Singapore study didn't like the fact that content only dealt with Muslims. Samples of verbatims are contained in Table 6.11.

Table 6.8
Aspects of SVI Commercials Most Liked

	London Sample (N=105)		Singapore Sample (N=328)	
	N	%	N	%
Tone/Point of View/Style	32	30.5	113	34.5
Friendly/happy/positive/uplifting	16		31	
"Normal" people/diverse, different people	9		35	
Objective/realistic	7		42	
Soothing music	0		5	
Overall Concept/Information Content	17	16.2	40	12.2
Good effort/good faith/good idea/ well done	10		17	
Information/content/learning	6		14	
The story	1		0	
Sharing personal experiences	0		9	
Information About Muslims	17	16.2	67	20.4
About successful Muslims/positive	6		23	
Equality/acceptance/respect for Muslims	2		17	
Muslims free/free to practice Islam	6		13	
Appropriate for Muslim countries	1		1	
Will help ease Muslim life after 9/11	1		6	
The teacher/classroom	1		3	
Fluent in English	0		2	
The student TV reporter	0		1	
The doctor	0		1	
Information about the United States	18	17.1	39	11.9
U.S. tolerance/respect	7		25	
Opportunities for other people in U.S.	5		10	
U.S. opportunities/successes/freedom	4		0	
U.S. image after 9/11	1		0	
Changed U.S. image	1		4	
Negative Comments	25	23.8	69	21.0
Nothing/"cheesy"/dislike/skeptical/no comment	25		45	
Blank (no answer)	0		21	
Too short	0		3	

Question: What did you like about the videos?

Several findings point to the presence of a generalized negative and cynical reaction to the spots. "First impressions" among more than half of the respondents characterized the content as not

Table 6.9
Sample Verbatims of Most Liked Aspects

Tone/Point of View/ Style:

The heart-warming approach towards the sensitive issue of a religion that has been misinterpreted by 9/11. Student from Singapore study.

It's simple and gives hints of hope and nice background music. Student from Singapore study.

It shows the bright sides and successful cases. Student from London study.

All the people are happy to live in the U.S. They are treated in a good way. Student from the London study.

Overall Concept and Information Content:

It conveys a message that everyone is free to practice their own religion and everyone is friendly, happy and tolerant towards one another. Student from Singapore study.

The fact that it sends out a positive message. It assures that anyone of any religion, especially Muslims, will have no problems nor will they be discriminated. It reassures those who have intentions of moving to U.S. permanently. Student from Singapore study.

Showed the truth of what really happens between different races, religions. Able to live and work together in a friendly environment. Student from Singapore study.

I think that it is a great message. Student from London study.

It is shown in good faith. Student from the London study.

Information About Muslims:

Rather surprised to see a number of Muslims who could actually speak rather fluent English. Felt that it is a good thing as it shows that their education is changing for the better. Student from Singapore study.

Hear a Muslim's opinion of living and working in America. Student from London study.

The reports/reportage of Muslim people. Student from London study.

Information About the United States:

As I said, to see the tolerance among different cultures. Student from London study.

I like how Americans help foreign people, and the respect that Americans give to them. Student from London study.

Negative Comments:

Not much - cheesy. Student from London study.

They were short, not too much information was given. Student from London study.

Table 6.10
Aspects of SVI Commercials Most Disliked

	London Sample (N=105)		Singapore Sample (N=328)	
	N	%	N	%
<u>Lack Believability</u>	<u>69</u>	<u>67.5</u>	<u>108</u>	<u>33.0</u>
Misleading/false/not real	35		36	
One-side/biased	23		28	
Too good to be true/too positive	6		38	
Skeptical	5		3	
Hypocritical	0		2	
People seem like actors	0		1	
<u>Specific Content</u>	<u>10</u>	<u>9.5</u>	<u>46</u>	<u>14.0</u>
The ending (from American people)	2		0	
Only about Muslims/Islam	2		22	
Only about religion	2		1	
Children's hospital	1		0	
That Americans are friendly	1		0	
Muslim women with heads covered	1		0	
U.S. too strong/dominant	1		0	
Only a small sample/minority of Muslims	0		10	
Only about successful/wealthy Muslims	0		6	
Lack of Caucasian Muslims	0		2	
Text/supers in video are hard to read	0		2	
People speak only in English	0		1	
Need more attractive characters	0		1	
Need better video production	0		1	
<u>Strategy/Approach/Format</u>	<u>7</u>	<u>6.7</u>	<u>30</u>	<u>9.1</u>
Seems like advertising/propaganda/PR	6		26	
Why was this (video) done?	1		0	
Too much talking	0		4	
"Everything" Disliked	3	2.9	0	0.0
Nothing Disliked	9	8.6	80	24.4
<u>Other</u>	<u>0</u>	<u>0.0</u>	<u>64</u>	<u>19.5</u>
Blank (no answer)	0		46	
Boring	0		9	
Very long	0		8	
Too short	0		1	

Question: What did you dislike about the videos?

Table 6.11
Sample Verbatims of Most Disliked Aspects

Lack of Believability:

Find it rather hard to believe that all the people in the videos are actually on such good terms with one another since there was a fixed mindset implanted in my mind that Muslims and Americans are always waging wars and causing suffering to the people and countries connected to them. Student from Singapore study.

Showing only specific people and only showing one side of their life but not the complete picture. Student from Singapore study.

It's obvious that it's a message meant to brainwash people into believing everything is just fine and dandy. Student from Singapore study.

It's misleading. Muslims are consistently harassed in the U.S. and have to go through special registration. Student from London study.

Again maybe the people were chosen specifically, it was not done on the streets with any strangers. Student from the London study.

Strategy/Approach/Format:

It is a propaganda of American culture. Student from Singapore study.

It feels very fake—like a kind of "Americans are nice people and love the Muslims" advertisement. Student from Singapore study.

I feel it's sort of advertising. Student from London survey.

Other:

Too slow and boring. Student from Singapore study.

The video only shows or dissembles about the Muslims, why not other religions? Student from London study.

Showing strong attitude to religious behavior. Only one view. Student from London study.

believable. Additionally, very few specific elements of the commercials were mentioned. This finding suggests a more global reaction to the content on the part of the viewer, rather than an objection to a particular statement or visual element, as is so often the case with commercial advertising copy tests.

Conclusion

The quasi-experimental data and copy tests reported in this chapter show that, after viewing the Shared Values Initiative commercials:

- Students were more likely to believe Muslims are fairly treated in the United States;
- Students had more positive attitudes toward the United States government and its people;
- Muslim students were more likely than Christians and other students to believe that Muslims are fairly treated in the United States, and their attitudes toward the United States government and its people also showed more improvement.

The copy test results showed that most of the students were able to play back a main message in the videos—that the United States is tolerant toward Muslims. In addition, a third to half of the students reported that:

- the commercials are believable to them and others;
- it is appropriate for the United States to air them in Muslim countries; and
- the commercials are an effective tool for communicating with Muslims.

Interestingly, European students in the study showed less favorable attitudes toward the United States than those from other parts of the world. Those who had visited the United States were more skeptical about the effectiveness of the spots than were others. This latter finding suggests that the commercials have the most influence on those least familiar the United States. Women—the primary target audience for the spots, according to Charlotte Beers—felt more strongly than men that the campaign represented an effective tool for the United States in its attempts to build bridges with the Muslim world.

Although the SVI commercials were effective in improving perceptions of the United States, their credibility might have been enhanced even more had they not been so one-sided. The commercials, which contained only scenes of happy Muslims living freely in the United States, may have conflicted with students' memories of news reports of Muslims as the objects of derision and sometimes violence in the aftermath of September 11. It would have been interesting to assess international student reaction had the State Department made the content more two-sided, addressing the issues of highly publicized yet relatively isolated incidents of Muslim mistreatment and providing some explanation of U.S. policy regarding Israel and Palestine.

As noted earlier in this chapter, one has to be cautious about generalizing these results beyond the laboratory, because the subjects themselves are college students and, thus, may not be representative of the populations in their home countries. However, to the extent that these students represent the next generation of world leaders in business and government, the data reported here may provide unique and valuable insights regarding the effectiveness of televised commercial messages.

Chapter Endnotes

[1] The authors' students also assisted in conducting the research described in this chapter. In July 2003 in London, Amanda Taylor was a primary assistant. In May 2004 in London, Alanna Bradley, Karen Brown and Maura Mollet assisted in the data collection. Dr. Fullerton's doctoral advisee, Matt Hamilton, conducted the Singapore study in March 2004 as part of his dissertation. See Matthew Hamilton, "Globalization and Anti-Americanism: A study of Singaporean college students" (Doctoral dissertation, Oklahoma State University, August, 2005), *Dissertation Abstracts International*, 66 (02), p. 395. Professor Kevin Keenan administered the study in Cairo.

[2]A disclosure of the funding source is provided so that readers know that the research was conducted independently—free from the influence of any governmental or political organization.

[3]Alice Kendrick and Jami Fullerton, "Advertising as public diplomacy: Attitude change among international audiences," *Journal of Advertising Research* 44 (2004): 297-311.

[4]Lawrence Pintak, "Dangerous delusions: Advertising nonsense about advertising America," University of Michigan, 27 August 2004, available online at www.publicdiplomacy.org/32.htm.

[5]Jack Haskins and Alice Kendrick, *Successful Advertising Research Methods* (Chicago: NTC Books, 1993).

[6]C. W. Yuen, "Leninism, Asian culture and Singapore," in *Asian Profile* (June 1999).

Additional reading about how to measure advertising effectiveness:

Babbie, E. R. *The practice of social research,* 6th ed. (Belmont, CA: Wadsworth, 1992).

Campbell, D. T. and J. C. Stanley, *Experimental and quasi-experimental designs and research,* (Skokie, IL: Rand McNally, 1963).

Haskins, Jack B., "A precise notational system for planning and analysis," *Evaluation Review,* Vol. 5, Issue 1, (1981) 33-50.

Haskins, Jack B., *How to evaluate mass communication.* (New York: Advertising Research Foundation, 1968).

Haskins, Jack B. and Alice Kendrick, *Successful Advertising Research Methods,* (Chicago: NTC Books, 1993).

Chapter 7

Advertising: A Weapon for the War on Terrorism?

The evidence presented in this book strongly suggests that advertising could be an effective weapon in the war on terrorism. Should the U.S. government use it? In this final chapter, we address this question after reviewing the Shared Values Initiative campaign and lessons to be learned from it. We also provide a number of suggestions for improving the government's public diplomacy programs.

Whom Under Secretary of State for Public Diplomacy and Public Affairs Charlotte Beers left Washington in March 2003, the Shared Values Initiative programs were immediately discontinued. Those now in the State Department cringe when the topic is mentioned. Public diplomacy practitioners and scholars continue to lambaste SVI and the idea of using advertising as a weapon in the war on terrorism. The official account is that SVI failed.

However, research presented in Chapter 5 and Chapter 6 of this book suggest that SVI may have worked. A case study conducted by an independent research firm in Indonesia reported very positive results in terms of message distribution, awareness and understanding. Experimental research that we conducted revealed that the SVI spots were capable of improving attitudes toward America among international young people.

So the question becomes: If communication campaigns like SVI have the potential to be effective, what went wrong in 2002 and what can be done in the future to make similar public diplomacy programs work better?

A host of problems associated with SVI—from lack of political support to lack of adequate test-marketing—have been identified in this book. However, from each problem emerges an opportunity to improve public diplomacy programs in the future. In this final chapter, the problems will be summarized and a list of recommendations will be offered.

The Politics of Politics

What Beers attempted to do in Washington was so unusual relative to traditional public diplomacy that, even if the message, medium and delivery had been flawless, some bureaucrats still would have condemned it.

She lacked political clout to combat such naysayers. Her staff was not skilled in mass communication techniques. Arguments over labels such as "propaganda," "advertising" and "selling" devalued and marginalized the effort. The inability of Beers' team to articulate the objectives of SVI and, therefore, set the standard for success among the public, press and politicians ultimately doomed the program.

Culture Clash

Beers faced enormous obstacles when she went to Washington in 2001. She had to manage her staff, sell her ideas to her counterparts in government and win the trust and support of the Washington press corps. Her replacement, Margaret Tutwiler, lasted less than six months. Beers stayed 17 months working diligently at her assignment of telling America's story abroad.

The press corps, taking some of its cues from long-term State

Department bureaucrats and other government officials, never warmed up to the idea of an advertising executive in public diplomacy. Some predicted that her lack of Washington know-how and her unwillingness to play political games would hurt her.

Former United States Information Agency staffer Nancy Snow said Beers "would be eaten alive by the bureaucratic lifers in the foreign policy establishment."[1] *AdWeek's* Washington Bureau Chief Wendy Melillo said, "Inside the State Department, Beers was surrounded by elitist snobs and diplomatic purists who didn't want their reputation, or the country's, sullied by marketing jargon."[2] Both statements proved true in the end.

The people and powers in Washington never embraced Beers' progressive style of public diplomacy. This hurt SVI and her other programs. With the exception of Secretary of State Colin L. Powell and former Ambassador Christopher Ross (see Chapter 4), it is difficult to find anyone who will speak positively about Beers and her work. And, as history has now shown, Powell's own lack of political clout within the Bush administration hurt his chances of promoting his own programs.

Client (a.k.a. Embassy) Buy-in Is a Must

Lack of cooperation from the embassies also hurt the ability of SVI to achieve its goals. Egypt's unwillingness to embrace SVI made other governments hesitant to allow the campaign on their state-owned television stations. Without the support of the U.S. ambassadors in Arab countries, SVI had little hope of gaining access to the people of those countries.

Some may claim that the business model cannot and should not apply to foreign affairs. However, in some respects, embassies are to the State Department what franchises are to a chain retail organization. Retail chain store owners work together with their corporate headquarters to develop strategy for the geographically far-flung ads that support their franchises. As "branches" of the U.S.

Department of State, embassies around the world are in a similar position to contribute to, as well as line up behind, an effort with "CEO" support intended to help their cause.

In the case of SVI, this crucial "client buy-in" apparently never happened. The failure to obtain internal commitment did as much to compromise SVI's chances for success as any outside phenomenon might have.

Communication inconsistencies sometimes arise in a franchise organization—for instance, not all restaurants adopt the new company logo simultaneously and for a time appear out of "sync" with each other. In the corporate world, a swift resolution of the problem is usually achieved. It would be poor business strategy to do otherwise, to not appear integrated, of "one voice," or coordinated.

Yet in the case of SVI, the lack of shared strategic values for the campaign was never overcome. Regardless of whose responsibility it was to coordinate the necessary embassy and State Department buy-in for SVI, Beers herself has said that the unwillingness of embassies to promote SVI and the refusal of state-run media to air it was "simply unacceptable."[3]

Communicating about Communication

Another significant obstacle was the State Department's lack of expertise in the fundamentals of communication.

Beers frequently mentioned the difficulty in working with staffers who knew little about communication theory and research. She organized training sessions for information officers who worked with the international media.

Despite their jobs in public affairs, many of them apparently had never been schooled in the basics of mass communication and media relations. Perhaps this obstacle was created, in part, when the U.S. Information Agency was dismantled and communication jobs became part of the State Department.

The P-word

There was a time when the word "propaganda" simply meant the dissemination of ideas. But today the word has taken on a negative connotation, and it incites suspicion, distrust, distortion and deception.

Were the SVI commercials propaganda? Of course, that depends on how one defines the term. Instead, it is better to focus on the content and ask whether it seriously distorts reality or is false.

Unfortunately, none of the critics who labeled SVI propaganda took the time to systematically study its content. And, unfortunately, many who hear the word propaganda immediately assume the worst or stop listening.

Stereotypes, which on the one hand are invaluable facilitators of efficient communication, can also serve as damaging labels. This appears to have been the case with the assignment of the propaganda label to SVI. In the same way that the ultimate insult of a congressional budget item is to call it "pork," one of the most damaging words that anyone could associate with a piece of communication is propaganda. Because of the unsavory connotations that are assigned to anything labeled propaganda, the creator of the message in question is automatically on the defensive—not an enviable position in public diplomacy, or any arena for that matter.

SVI was immediately dismissed as propaganda by nay-sayers around the world, whose quotes became easy sound-bite prey for journalists. The swift and negative reaction in the press had a pre-emptive effect on whatever the State Department might have put together in the way of support for its months of work.

The A-word

Possibly even more damaging to the SVI effort than the label "propaganda" was the term "advertising."

Beers called the spots "mini-documentaries." The vignettes of Muslim life in America lasted about two minutes each and were run on both state-owned media and pan-Arab satellite channels during paid commercial breaks. They were produced by one of the world's leading advertising agencies, distributed according to an advertising media plan, and when results came in, they were compared with both product and public service advertising campaigns running in the United States.

Here was an icon of American advertising, producing public service-type videos as part of a much larger and otherwise nonadvertising effort to communicate with peoples of the world, going out of her way to avoid the term "advertising."

Why such a fuss about whether SVI was advertising? We struggled with the question. One reading is that Beers' counterparts in Washington cautioned her against using terms such as advertising when referring to public diplomacy. While Powell seemed comfortable in using marketing terms when he spoke about the image of the United States, others obviously were not.

Mary Matalin, an adviser to Vice President Dick Cheney, said in February 2002 that Beers' emphasis on branding "has cast this patina over the whole operation."[4] Later in a December 2002 presentation about SVI to the National Press Club, Beers caught and corrected herself as though she had been told not to use the word advertising: "Here is what we call a collage, a summary of advertising messages—I used the 'a-word.' I shouldn't have done that—a summary of messages prepared for communication … "[5]

This slip suggests that Beers' believed the word advertising was most appropriate in describing SVI—but she was avoiding its use. Perhaps there was a conscious decision within the administration to avoid terms that could be associated with advertising and marketing in response to the deluge of cynical reaction that the press was delivering. Apparently members of the media found it disturbing that something as serious as public diplomacy could be linked with something as trivial as advertising.

Whether or how the State Department could have inoculated its

SVI campaign against being summarily dismissed as propaganda, or as advertising, could be a subject of debate among communication scholars and advertising professionals for some time.

Advertising Could Use Some PR

As discussed earlier, the skepticism and cynicism expressed by SVI critics often took the form of deliberate juxtapositions of marketing communication and public diplomacy. These quotes included "From Uncle Ben's to Uncle Sam"[6] and "If we can't effectively fight anthrax, I guess it's reassuring to know we can always win the war on dandruff."[7]

Future public diplomacy practitioners need to appreciate that such ad-bashing, regardless of how sound a strategy might underpin a campaign effort, is virtually inevitable. Beyond the unconditional assertion that advertising did not belong in the realm of public diplomacy, some critics were quick to point out the obvious—that advertising would be unable to "win the hearts and minds" in the Muslim world. This criticism is rather extraordinary when one considers the almost impossible standard to which advertising was being held: SVI would be a failure if it did not succeed in reversing all negative attitudes toward America.

Most public diplomacy experts would agree that exchange programs such as Fulbright represent the gold standard in terms of efforts to foster understanding and respect among individuals from different cultures. But none would suggest that international exchanges would completely rectify the U.S. image problem abroad—that a limited a number of students or professionals trading places for a few months could do it all.

So why were expectations for advertising so high? It appears that the unrealistic expectations among many critics belied their unfamiliarity with what advertising can realistically accomplish.

One of the responsibilities of an advertising agency is to demonstrate to clients how advertising benefits their products or brands. In her role as Under Secretary, Beers actually was the client, and therefore acquired the services of McCann-Erickson to plan and produce advertising to achieve her objectives.

However, because the U.S. government had no previous experience with activities like SVI, the more difficult task for her became the need to defend her ideas and sell the value of advertising to very skeptical audiences—her colleagues at the State Department and beyond. Because she was new to public diplomacy and because she was flamboyant, Beers was hampered in her efforts to educate and persuade many of those around her that her ideas had merit.

Shared Values Needed Shared Objectives

Why are we advertising?

This disarmingly simple question is at the top of every strategic brief at major agencies. Its answer drives all subsequent strategic and tactical decisions, such as which part of a market will be targeted, which geographic area emphasized, which media selected and which message communicated. It appears that this aspect of Advertising 101 was not sufficiently addressed when SVI was undertaken. Judging from the dissension that ensued after the campaign was launched, a clear objective was not shared by all.

Beers set her sights on relatively modest communication objectives—awareness and knowledge—both toward the bottom of the communication hierarchy of effects. However, others appeared to have very different ideas about what SVI should accomplish. The phrase "winning the hearts and minds" of the "Muslim world" was repeatedly used in headlines and articles about the campaign. These goals imply attitude change and are higher on the "effects ladder."

Communication research tells us that many more barriers confront the communicator who tries to "win hearts" than does the communicator who attempts to achieve recall and recognition—good or bad—for her message. Regardless, later experimental research, as described in Chapter 6, revealed that the SVI spots were capable of improving attitudes toward America—maybe SVI could have won "hearts and minds" after all.

In December 2002, Beers told a group of businesswomen in Dallas that "any discussion," including criticism and parody by Islamic extremists, would be considered a sign of success given her fundamental goal of "starting a dialogue" on the subject. Using a multi-media presentation, she confidently displayed parodied images of the SVI print ads, reportedly produced by an anti-U.S. organization and posted in public places in Pakistan.

Although parody is by no means the highest form of communications flattery, it is an indicator of campaign success. Groups don't parody ads they think others will not recognize, and in order to be recognized widely, the original intended message has to have been distributed and acknowledged widely. If awareness of the SVI campaign was a goal, as Beers repeatedly stated, then parody would indeed be considered at least a crude measure of success.

Looking at the different and sometimes conflicting goals for SVI among various groups, including those at the State Department, it is no wonder the campaign was branded a failure. Without an understanding of what would constitute success, the program could not succeed.

Source/Message Issues

Copy test research on SVI showed that there were weaknesses within the commercials, including their overly positive one-sided approach and emphasis on the United States as the source of the message.

Was a Single-edged Message a Double-edged Sword?

By far the biggest criticism of the SVI commercials among those who participated in the advertising copy tests described in Chapter 6 was their one-sided approach. Even those whose attitudes toward the United States improved as the result of viewing the ads were likely to say they had reservations about whether the content was entirely true. Specifically they wondered whether negative information about Muslim mistreatment in the United States after 9/11 had been purposefully omitted to strengthen the sell.

It was beyond the scope of the copy test studies to create and test alternative versions of SVI containing a more balanced or two-sided message. However, persuasion scholars have amassed a considerable body of research that suggests that even a mild inoculation against message rejection, such as acknowledging that another point of view might be held, can be enough to significantly predispose the viewer to accept the intended message.

The U.S. Government as 'Credible Messenger'

Many who criticized SVI contend that the U.S. government is not a credible messenger. They assert that lack of source credibility may cause the target audience to dismiss, ignore or even resent the incoming message.

While the U.S. government may not be the most popular entity among Arab and Muslim governments, research suggests that the American people are well liked around the world. Beers' choice to create an ad "from the American people" and the Council of American Muslims for Understanding (CAMU) appeared to be accepted and largely unquestioned by the target audience. This is an interesting aspect of the campaign.

Given the fact that most Americans were not aware of SVI, the choice to attribute the ads to the American people may raise some ethical questions. Does using taxpayer money give the government the right to name the "American people" as a source of the message? Furthermore, does an organization that was arguably funded by the State Department need to identify itself as such? Should such questions even be asked of public diplomacy messages?

The news media did not raise issues of source attribution, nor did the participants in the advertising copy test. If the U.S. government sponsors campaigns such as SVI in the future, it will be interesting to see whether and how such sponsorship is reflected in the message.

Mass communication research suggests that over time the message is remembered, but the source is often forgotten. Perhaps source credibility and the credibility of the U.S. government is not as much of a liability as some claim.

Opportunities Abound for Numerous Messengers

American business and industry have a huge stake in improving America's image for a variety of reasons, not the least of which is the potential impact it has on sales of their products in global markets.

Organizations such as Business for Diplomatic Action are forming and are willing to take action on behalf of Brand America. However, as valuable and energetic as private companies can be, they are not well equipped, even together, to tackle the job of public diplomacy comprehensively.

The ideal model, as Beers suggested, would use the private-sector and be coordinated by the U.S. government, which would provide assistance with funding and overcoming red-tape such as visa restrictions.

Pretesting + Pilot-testing = Insurance

Although pretesting and pilot-testing commercials before a campaign is launched can be expensive and time-consuming, they can identify problems before they become diplomatic crises. Some of the problems associated with the SVI media plan could have been identified and perhaps remedied.

Even corporate advertising executives reading this book might question whether it would be realistic to run a small-scale campaign prior to the full-on launch, but advertisers who are willing to devote the time and money to such efforts reap the benefits of an early read on actual market response.

On the other hand, there is also the possibility that even if a pilot test of SVI had been executed, it might have triggered negative publicity, which in turn could have compromised SVI's chances of a full rollout.

Delivery Issues

Campaign effectiveness depends in large part on whether messages are delivered at the right time and through the appropriate channels. A number of issues with SVI involved the ability of the media to deliver the campaign as initially planned. A larger question is whether a long-term communication strategy should be employed for public diplomacy programs, such as SVI, in order to enhance their prospects for success.

Did They Deliver?

McCann-Erickson placed the media buys for the SVI campaign. The planned exposure in each country was at a level adequate to achieve communication effectiveness among the target audience.

However, no post-buy analyses were found in the agency documents, so it can be assumed that none was conducted. It is difficult to know if the agency numbers are accurate and if the SVI messages were delivered as scheduled. Some countries that appeared on the media plan later refused to run the spots. How could it have been determined if state-owned systems in Indonesia, Malaysia, Pakistan and Kuwait ran all the spots that were ordered, without post-campaign verification?

Global marketers face this problem frequently, particularly in underdeveloped countries where media audience measurements are less sophisticated and state-owned media systems less dependable than media outlets in the United States. This is important because if the ads did not run as placed, no matter how brilliant the creative execution, SVI could fail due to lack of distribution. If the target audience does not have a chance to see the message, the message will not have an impact.

Creativity with Media

The media landscape in the Arab and Muslim world has experienced tremendous change because of new technologies like the Internet and satellite. Reaching audiences in authoritarian countries was once almost impossible without governmental cooperation, but now can be achieved through new channels.

Mamoun Fandy recommended use of mother-tongue media such as the Paris newspaper *Le Monde* to communicate with North African countries whose governments would not allow SVI in their own media.[8] This idea might have had some merit, although such distribution would not have been nearly as efficient as in-country media in reaching the intended target.

In-country expertise is vital in understanding media usage patterns in the rapidly changing developing world. Creative approaches to media delivery will be necessary to reach Arab and Muslim audiences in the future.

Timing Is Everything

Two time-related apertures, or openings, factored in what could be considered both successes and failures of SVI.

State Department officials and others point to what they considered a critical delay in finalizing and launching the campaign. The need to re-shoot some of the video or greatly edit existing tape in order to remove specific religious references was the result of the Justice Department's concern about blurring the lines of church and state.

The four months that were lost have been characterized as a precious window of opportunity within which America did not fully capitalize on post-9/11 world sympathy. By the time SVI ran, it was too late in some senses because other developments had taken center stage, including the run-up to the war in Iraq. The State Department's resources and attention were needed for the Iraq situation. The prospect of war easily trumped SVI.

The fact that SVI was delayed by four months created an aperture of its own, as the campaign would eventually run during the religious season of Ramadan. Muslim families spend more time together and watch more television during Ramadan, a fact that indirectly contributed to greater audience exposure to the messages.

Might there have been some sort of aperture during which State Department officials, especially U.S. ambassadors, would have been more open to the concept of SVI, and consequently supported the effort more vigorously? If such an aperture existed, it appears it was not successfully leveraged.

Effective Advertising Is a Long-Term Investment

Decades of research on brand equity and advertising econometrics demonstrate that advertising adds value to a brand, and that such value is sustained and enhanced by maintaining the presence of effective brand messages over time. This book was not conceived as a 'Brand America' guide, but it is impossible to discuss SVI without acknowledging that it represented a first effort to do something—and a single effort only.

In advertising parlance, SVI was a one-shot campaign—delivered to one audience at a single point in time. Despite signs that the campaign had its intended effect among the primary target audience, no subsequent efforts have been undertaken.

Practically all of the programs initiated by Beers have disappeared from the public diplomacy menu. Web sites containing SVI materials have been taken down. The extraordinary difficulty we encountered when requesting SVI materials is indicative of how reluctant the State Department is to revisit Beers' programs and to have scholars examine them to inform future public diplomacy initiatives.

But why?

Asked to reflect on the reality that her programs were not continued soon after she resigned, Beers said she believed it was lack of motivation and leadership on the part of State Department officials.

The Alternative Is to do Nothing

Citizens of predominantly Muslim countries are fed a steady diet of news and programming that consistently casts the United States in a negative light. The American story may not be told in the Arab and Muslim world unless the United States provides quality messages and, in some cases, its own media vehicles. *Hi* Magazine, Radio Sawa and Al Hurra are examples of this strategy.

Beers understood that silence on the part of the United States was extremely dangerous in a media-saturated world where ample negative stories about America are available for broadcast. Her recommendation to provide quality programming to Arab and Muslim media in the form of mini-documentaries and eventually more lengthy programs is a strategy that deserves consideration.

Receiver Issues

By public diplomacy standards, SVI used unconventional strategies to reach an unconventional audience. Beers defined her goal as reaching "the people," not the "elites," and more specifically defined the target audience as women—"the mothers and teachers."

Not everyone in Washington agreed with her approach to public diplomacy. But mass media theories such as two-step flow suggest that campaigns targeting family opinion leaders such as women can be quite effective.

Is advertising really that different from one-on-one public diplomacy?

In his book, *In Defense of Advertising,* Jerry Kirkpatrick[9] points out that there are only two factors that differentiate personal selling from advertising: advertising is delivered to many people at once and is carried through a medium, as opposed to being presented in person.

No one questions whether it is appropriate for ambassadors and other diplomats to 'sell' U.S. policies and ideals to the governments and citizens of other countries. That's their job. Yet it is terribly disconcerting to some that such informational and persuasive activities would be launched on a much larger scale through advertising.

Beers understood this concept well. She continually emphasized the importance of going past the elites to speak with "the people." She knew that using mass media was the best way to reach "the people." In an interview on National Public Radio a full year after she left the State Department, she emphasized this point again and said that the governmental elites and leaders in the country knew very little about their people, or what their concerns were.[10]

One of the strategies for SVI was to influence women in the hope that they would spread the positive word about America to those within their spheres of influence, including young men. Mass media researchers call this the two-step flow theory of mass communication, a phenomenon of opinion or thought leaders passing along information and ideas introduced by media. Two-step flow can be used to explain the success of many commercial and public service campaigns. Beers' knowledge of the power of women to influence members of their households was evident in her SVI plan as well as other communication efforts, such as Rewards for Justice.

Targeting opinion leaders in the Arab and Muslim World such as clerics could also be considered. In traditional societies, religious leaders have a great impact on their communities. Aiming SVI-type messages at community leaders, who will pass the messages on to others in society over whom they have influence, may be potentially more powerful than targeting people directly. This strategy should not be confused with targeting "elites" in the country, such as government officials, academics and the aristocracy, who in such cultures often have little interaction with the broader society.

Recommendations

Now that the story of America's first advertising campaign to the Arab and Muslim world has been more fully told, we offer a number of recommendations. Some of these suggestions echo the sentiments of other writers on the subject and some are new in view of information presented in this book.

1. *Reorganize the public diplomacy function and hire information officers with knowledge in the field of communication.* As many before us have suggested, the United States Information Agency should be returned to its previous independence, outside of the State Department. In addition, that agency and the State Department both should hire information officers that are specifically skilled in the field of communication. Individuals with degrees in advertising, public relations and marketing communications might be better candidates than those with degrees in public policy and foreign affairs.

   Ideally candidates would have both—communication training and diplomatic experience. Seek out experienced managers who work in advertising and public relations firms, corporate and nonprofit communication departments and the media. America has an abundance of talented communication managers. The U.S. government should leverage this talent.

2. *Put a "communication czar" in charge of public diplomacy.* Elevate the current Under Secretary position to a level with

direct access to the President of the United States. The political obstacles that beset Beers must be overcome. This person should be someone who has the skill to navigate Washington politics, but, more importantly, one who understands communications and international audiences.

3. *Get the ambassadors on board with public diplomacy decisions.* U.S. ambassadors are the vital link to international governments and societies. Without their support and project buy-in, public diplomacy programs will never reach their target. The embassies should not be given an easy option of opting out once a decision about a program has been made.

4. *Acknowledge that public diplomacy is not 100% dependent on foreign policy.* Perhaps public diplomacy aimed at regular citizens in other countries need not include issues directly related to U.S. foreign policy. Other messages can resonate with non-Americans, such as dispelling misperceptions about America and emphasizing the good work that America does in foreign lands through aid and humanitarian programs. Opening communication lines is one way to connect with the people in the Arab and Muslim world, regardless of foreign policy decisions.

At a minimum, if communication lines are open, hostilities may be reduced and controversial U.S. governmental policy, when it affects the citizens of another country, may be more easily tolerated. It is important to consider that some experts on al Qaeda believe that the 9/11 attacks would have happened regardless of the U.S. government's position in the Palestinian/Israeli crisis. Everyone knows that all products aren't perfect in all aspects, but they continue to be sold to certain segments who find appeal in and benefit from them. In this same way, recognize that public diplomacy won't win the hearts and minds of everyone in the Arab and Muslim world, but there is a majority for whom aspects of America's story will be quite appealing, informative and persuasive.

5. *Think creatively about public diplomacy—try nonconventional approaches.* Don't be afraid to do things differently than they have been done in the past. Creative thinkers seem to be in short supply at all levels of government. Look outside, as Secretary Powell did, and bring people to Washington who are well-known creative problem-solvers. They may not dress like others in Washington, D.C., but they will surprise you with their insight and fresh thinking.

6. *Use research expertise at all levels—go outside Washington, D.C., if necessary.* Universities and the private sector contain an abundance of resources for all types of communication functions, but particularly in the area of research. Communication may seem too soft to be a science, but in fact, well-conceived, well-executed research can enhance the success of most communication campaigns. Consider creating a "Manhattan Project" for public diplomacy that brings together top communication researchers and strategists from around the world in an environment where they can work freely to tackle America's image problem.

7. *Consider private sector initiatives supported by government coordination and cash.* The private sector is ready and willing to help the government improve America's image, since this may enhance their business around the world. Organizations like Business for Diplomatic Action have

already developed public diplomacy initiatives that can work, but they need the financial and organizational support of the U.S. government. Perhaps the government should be a silent partner in these efforts, but it must be involved in order to overcome the monetary and bureaucratic obstacles that exist in dealing with foreign publics.

8. *Manage expectations in Washington and in the press.* There are no magic bullets in mass communication. Articulate the objectives of each communication program in advance, measure the results and promote the successes when achieved.

9. *Commit to the program for the long-term.* Reversing the tidal wave of anti-American sentiment that exists in the 21st century will not happen quickly. Communication programs aimed at this mission must be put in place and supported over the long term. A consistent message and communication program that stretches beyond presidential terms is required.

10. *Do not exclude advertising as a possible weapon in the war on terrorism.* The evidence reported in this study strongly suggests that it would be a mistake to summarily exclude advertising or any other marketing tool that may enhance public diplomacy efforts. More research on the use of advertising as a tool of public diplomacy is, of course, necessary. But the empirical data from the post-campaign survey in Indonesia and our quasi-experimental research strongly suggest that advertising may be an effective tool in the war on terrorism. As former Secretary of State Colin Powell pointed out, "We've got to get creative people from

the most creative media society on the face of the earth to put their time, attention and mind power to this."[11]

Finally, we hope that this book has alerted Americans and the U.S. government to the importance of creating a meaningful dialogue with our global neighbors. In this post-9/11 world, even though people have become more interconnected through technology, they also have often become more separated through misunderstanding. Effective communication is one tool that can bring us together.

Chapter Endnotes

[1]Nancy Snow, email interview by the authors, 29 August 2005.

[2]Wendy Melillo, "Defending Beers," *Adweek,* 10 March 2003, p. 24.

[3]Charlotte Beers, phone interview by authors, 5 July 2005, Tulsa, OK.

[4]"From Uncle Ben's to Uncle Sam," *Economist,* Vol. 362 (23 February 2002), p. 70.

[5]Charlotte Beers, remarks to the National Press Club, Washington DC, 18 December 2002. Retrieved from http://www.state.gov/r/us/16269.htm on 3 November 2005.

[6]"From Uncle Ben's to Uncle Sam," *Economist.*

[7]Frank Rich, "Journal; How to Lose A War," *The New York Times,* 27 October 2001, sec. A, p. 19.

[8]Mamoun Fandy, telephone interview by authors, Tulsa, OK, 3 September 2005.

[9]Jerry Kirkpatrick, *In Defense of Advertising: Arguments from Reason, Ethical Egoism and Laissez Faire Capitalism* (Westport CT: Quorum Books, 1994).

[10]Bob Garfield, "Selling America," NPR radio interview with Charlotte Beers, 26 March 2004. Retrieved from http://www.onthemedia.org/transcripts/transcripts_032604_selling.html on 3 November 2005.

[11]Comment by Secretary of State Colin L. Powell before the Senate Foreign Relations Committee, October 25, 2001.

Story Boards for the Five Shared Values Initiative Television Spots

This appendix contains the story boards for the five Shared Values Initiative Television commercials. To view the actual spots themselves, visit www.osu-tulsa.okstate.edu/sharedvalues/. See Table 1.2 in Chapter 1 for more specific information about each spot.

Baker, pp. 218-220

Doctor, pp. 221-222

Teacher, pp. 223-224

Journalist, pp. 225-226

Firefighter, pp. 227-228

Baker
(continued on next page)

I believe the American people in general respect the Islamic faith. Muslims can practice their faith in totality here.

Hello my name is Abdul Hammuda, I am the owner of Tiger Lebanese bakery located here in Toledo, Ohio, the United States of America. We make the greatest pita bread in the nation. I was born and raised in Tripoli, Libya. I came to America to go to school.

After I graduated I really saw the great opportunity this country would have for me as a businessman. My wife is my right hand person.

My name is Shadia Hammuda. We are making mujaddara. It is lintel and rice with onion.

Baker
(continued from previous page)

The bakery was a much smaller place than you see today and I introduce some dishes from the African nation of Libya, Morocco and Tunisia, and that's how we grew.

My name is Ahmad Hammuda, I am studying pharmacy at the University of Toledo.

I have been very fortunate to have my children with me at the bakery.

My name is Leena Hammuda, I am a registered junior at the Toledo Islamic Academy.

Baker
(continued from previous page)

The Toledo Islamic Academy is the Islamic school, the first of its kind in the state of Ohio, and I was one of the co-founders of the school. We started with about fifty students, now we are from pre-k to high school.

Religious freedom here is something very important, and we see it practiced and no one ever bothered us. Living the straight path in America, I don't think is hard because it is a choice you have to make.

Since 9/11 we've had an overwhelming sense of support from our customers and clients.

America is a land of opportunity, of equality. We are happy to live here as Muslims and preserve our faith.

Doctor
(continued on next page)

There is a profound connection between medicine and Islam.

I mean through knowledge, you can improve not just medicine, but a lot of men.

My name is Dr. Zerhouni, I am the Director of the National Institute of Health in America, and I have been nominated to this position by President George Bush.

The mission of the National Institute of Health is to advance knowledge about the medical care and diseases that affect mankind.

Doctor
(continued from previous page)

There are eighteen thousand people working here in Washington and there are forty five thousand projects that the Institute funds throughout the world. When we develop a new treatment it is available worldwide, so it impacts on the health of everyone on earth.

I was born in Algeria, on the western side of Algeria in a small town called Nedroma. I became very interested in medicine because I had an uncle who was actually a radiologist. Well, I came in America in 1975. I was totally embraced by people here, my professors. You know, everybody told me we are all immigrants here, we are all from different places, and we all melt together and I love that, I really do.

The notion that science can improve health has been borne out in Islam for many centuries. Some of the best doctors in the history of the world have been Muslim doctors.

What I can tell Muslims around the world is the tolerance and support I've received myself is remarkable. I don't think that there is any other country in the world, where I think different people from different countries are accepted and welcomed as members of the society, as good citizens.

School Teacher
(continued on next page)

I decided to become a teacher because I enjoy talking to the kids, working with the children, more than anything.

My name is Rawia Ismail. I am a school teacher in public school in the United States of America.

I wear a hijab in the classroom where I teach. Children ask me a lot of questions. I've never had any child that thought it was weird or anything like that, and they like the fact, both them and their parents, that they are introduced to different culture.

I was born in Lebanon, in Beirut, Lebanon. We came to the United States in '84. Islam in the United States could be followed just as well as I can follow in my village where I was raised.

School Teacher
(continued from previous page)

In general it's very practical to practice Islam and live in U.S. My neighbors, they are fair minded and good people. So they are – they understand us.

I also teach my children in Saturday school, Islamic school. I teach the kids about an hour of religion and an hour of Arabic, and they have some lunch in between, and than we all do prayers together. This is something that I found to be an important way of life to me and my family. In my neighborhood all the non-Muslims, I see that they care a lot about their children's education, just as much as I do and about family values.

My neighbors have always been supportive, truly. I didn't quite see any prejudice anywhere in my neighborhood after the September 11.

I had to work at getting the kids to understand that most important that we should work on our similarities rather than our differences.

Journalist
(continued on next page)

To become a journalist, of course, you have to uphold truth. You have to be honest and you have to be objective, and all those values I've already learned. Hi, I am Devianti Faridz. I am a Master's student majoring in broadcast journalism at the University of Missouri in the United States. I was born in Bandoon, Indonesia.

The values of Islam that I have been taught ever since I was a child are the values that I have been exposed to here at school – honesty, truth, knowledge.

KOMU-TV is related to the University of Missouri. A majority of the students work as reporters, producers or anchors for news breaks here. So, while I am learning I can also work at a real television station. It is stressful, but that's part of the training. (Faridz on television: Good Morning I am Devianti Faridz, thanks for waking up with us.)

I am fortunate that I live in Columbia, Missouri, where there is a mosque. That enables me to gather with my Muslim friends and pray together, celebrate religious holidays together. So far the American students that I have met have respected my beliefs.

Journalist
(continued from previous page)

(Faridz on television: Nine miners have been trapped since Wednesday night.)

I hope to be able to go back home to Indonesia and become an objective journalist who can contribute to the betterment of society. We should embrace diversity and differences, and not be afraid of them.

It is nice to know that Americans are willing to understand more about Islam, and there is an opportunity for mutual understanding.

Firefighter
(continued on next page)

You get the call, you go. The job is about helping other people. They are relying on us and we are the first ones to help them right away. I am a paramedic for a fire department of New York.

I am a volunteer chaplain with the MT Police department. Those who are putting their lives on the line each and every day to protect the citizens of this nation. It is my responsibility to do whatever I can, whether that is offering counseling or spiritual guidance or words of acknowledgement of the hard work that they are doing.

I have co-workers who are Jewish, Christian, Hindu even, all different faiths. We get along fine. You know, we treat each other with respect. They have all been supportive of me since the 9/11 attack and I have been very grateful for that.

I have never gotten disrespected because I am a Muslim.

Firefighter
(continued from previous page)

I think Muslims in America have more freedom to work for Islam perhaps more than any other country that I have visited.

Presented by the Council of
American Muslims for Understanding

We are all brothers and sisters and here I am as a human taking care of another.

Don't Brand the U.S., Uncle Sam: The Backlash Against Charlotte Beers' America-Branding

By John Brown

Published online at www.CommonDreams.org, Monday, December 13, 2004. Reprinted here with permission.

In testimony before the House Budget Committee on March 15, 2001, Secretary of State Colin Powell announced: "I'm going to be bringing people into the public diplomacy function of the department who are going to change from just selling us in the old…way to really branding foreign policy, branding the department, marketing the department, marketing American values to the world."

The person Powell chose to lead his branding effort was Charlotte Beers, a 66-year old Texas-born marketing magician without diplomatic, political, or policy experience, who was appointed Under Secretary of State for Public Diplomacy and Public Affairs soon after 9/11. Known as "the queen of branding," Beers announced that she had "the most sophisticated brand assignment I have ever had." Her goal was to sell "the brand of the United States."

Seventeen Months

She lasted 17 months, resigning for "health reasons." The general consensus is that she did little, if anything, to "move the needle" of world public opinion more favorably toward the United States, criticized in numerous countries because of Bush's militaristic, unilateral policies. Her projects—including a widely dismissed magazine targeted at Muslim youth, a brochure on terrorism found to be simplistic, and much ridiculed videos showing Muslims the happy life of their co-religionists in America—came under intense criticism. They won't long be remembered. Beers's most lasting achievement will be seen in the negative. Branding was never everybody's favorite (it "suggests a huckster's sales pitch," says Chris Reidy of *The Boston Globe*), but during the Madison Avenue diva's brief appearance in Washington it became associated, much to its detriment, with her "ad" nauseam initiatives.

The anti-Beers-branding backlash comes from five sources.

From the Right

First, and recently, from the political right. There were criticisms of Beers's methods early on in the pages of the conservative *The Weekly Standard*, but the loudest reactionary voices against her came after Bush got reelected, in the pages of *The Wall Street Journal.*

On November 16, a *Journal* editorial lambasted the State Department's "misbegotten efforts to sell American values to the Middle East by way of a Madison-inspired ad campaign." "But the U.S.," it argues, "can't be sold as a 'brand,' like Cheerios." It blamed Secretary Powell for this failure "to take control of his department."

In the November 17 WSJ, Eliot Cohen, the well-known neoconservative, stated that "Condoleezza Rice must reinvent our public diplomacy, articulating abroad the values for which the U.S.

stands, using not the techniques of Madison Avenue executives (one of the failures of the first part of the administration) but speech rooted in America's history and politics."

and the Left

The second source of brand criticism is from the left, which had been after Ms. Beers from day-one, given her wealth, Republican connections, and Madison Avenue background. Its complaints about Beers's legacy are endless, and underscore a point not made by the pro-Bush right—that U.S. public diplomacy under the current administration has failed to take the consequences of unpopular policies into serious consideration. As Naomi Klein says in "Failure of Brand USA" (The Guardian, March 14, 2002): *"America's problem is not with its brand ... but with its product."*

Klein goes on to condemn branding, an enemy of "diversity and debate," which are "the lifeblood of liberty." Historically, she says, the "ugly flip side of politicians striving for brand consistency" are "centralized information, state-controlled media, re-education camps, purging of dissidents and much worse."

Pentagon Advisers

A third source of skepticism about Beers-era branding comes in a report of the Defense Science Board Task Force to the Pentagon that first appeared in September 2004 but was covered by the media only after the presidential election. The 102-page report, which drew extensive commentary, notes that:

Through the peak of mass marketing in the latter part of the 20th century, th[e] domination of private sector mass communications resources literally developed the power of Western popular culture and the growth of global brands.

It goes on to say, however, that:

the same factors that added to the power of the incumbent leaders and brands also provided opportunity for insurgent movements and insurgent companies—for fresh, cutting-edge and sharply differentiated competitors. Today, as a result of the global Information Revolution, private sector mass marketing is losing its relative power.

The report concludes that the U.S. must adopt the strategies and tactics of the insurgent, not the incumbent: waging a proactive, bold and effective U.S. strategic communication effort.

A conclusion that can be drawn from these observations is that twentieth-century branding a la Beers is an anachronism, an outdated method of dealing with the challenges American foreign policy faces in a new world of terror networks.

Foreign Policy Professionals

Criticisms of Ms. Beers's methods, many of them uttered sotto voce, were rampant among foreign policy professionals at the State Department during her brief tenure, including from former officers of the United States Information Agency (USIA), which was consolidated into the Department in 1999. A recent voice of dissatisfaction with her branding techniques comes from Richard Haass, who was Director of Policy Planning at the US Department of State during George W. Bush's first term and is now President of the Council on Foreign Relations. In an article that just appeared in Newsweek online, he stresses that business methods cannot be necessarily applied in government—or be useful for business itself. He cites as a example of misapplied business talent none other than Charlotte Beers, noting that:

Her attempts to improve America's image in the Arab and Muslim worlds through media spots depicting happy American Muslims fell flat. It is one thing to sell Uncle Ben's rice, another to sell Uncle Sam's foreign policy.

Haass goes on to note:

Why do so many people coming out of business run into trouble? In business, success can be measured by profits. How does one measure the quality of a public service...

No Way to Run a Business

The business community itself is a final source of Beers criticism. From the very day she took office, savvy articles in Advertising Age and Brandweek cast doubts about use of her branding to advance U.S. interests abroad. A group of business people concerned about America's declining overseas image—Business for Diplomatic Action—was incorporated in January 2004. Although the group doesn't use the term, "Brand America," it's not opposed to branding as such, which it feels U.S. government can't handle properly. *"Our experience is that when we try to do something with the government, it just turns into a pile of paper,"* the president of BDA, Keith Reinhard, says.

Yuri Radzievsky, CEO, GlobalWorks Group, in an "Open Letter to Charlotte Beers" (Brandweek, January 21, 2002), summarizes a viewpoint that many, no matter their political divergences or occupations, would not disagree with:

I believe in the power of communication. I was born in the Soviet Union, where the media, as in many Muslim parts of the world, was state-controlled. Our generation grew up questioning everything that purported, on TV or in print, to be factual. I remember commercials for a Western-made chocolate, branded as just the thing to have in your pocket when feeling hungry. To many truly hungry Russians, who couldn't afford bread, no less sweets, the message sounded terribly cynical. I grew up to hate the brand for showing us what we couldn't have. Let's not have America make the same mistake.

Public Diplomacy: What Have We Learned?

By Joe B. Johnson

Reproduced with the permission of the author and the Foreign Service Journal.

As the incoming Under Secretary for Public Diplomacy takes up our fragmented public diplomacy apparatus to face the most hostile world opinion climate in memory, he or she will no doubt hear about the "failed" Shared Values advertising campaign by Charlotte Beers.

After reviewing the 2002 Beers initiative, I am convinced that Shared Values' most important lessons have been hidden.

The fact is that the messages, which were researched and pre tested with target audience members, actually worked when State was able to place them in foreign media. The enterprise avoided the chief ailments of today's public diplomacy: poor use of research, insufficient planning, and spotty evaluation.

A Bit of History

After the attacks upon America on September 11, President Bush himself asked: "Why do they hate us?" Beers, a veteran Madison Avenue executive, turned to her disciplines in persuasive communication to respond.

Beers asked the Intelligence and Research Bureau to find out why publics aged 18 to 35 in Muslim nations regarded the U.S. with hostility. INR went beyond the opinion polls to find out how foreigners felt about American society, conducting some original research but also reviewing a broad swath of existing behavioral and commercial research.

The studies offered new insights. For example, a Roper poll of 35 nations showed that Muslims felt their dearest values—modesty, obedience, duty—were neglected in the U.S. Nearly all the research revealed that foreign Muslims sensed American hostility to them and their religion. However, the Roper study and others also showed that Muslims had little knowledge that values like faith, family and learning were also cherished by Western societies.

On that basis, Beers stated two objectives for a communication campaign: target a few countries to establish a mindset that Americans and Muslims share many values and beliefs; and demonstrate that America is not at war with Islam. The Secretary endorsed those objectives.

Beers' strategy relied on American Muslims telling about their lives in the U.S., free from oppression and surrounded by strong families. The campaign was built around five mini-documentaries featuring a student, a teacher, a New York firefighter and Dr. Elias Zerhouni, director of the National Institutes of Health. Each first-person account demonstrated one or more of those underappreciated values: family life, zeal for education and American respect for freedom of religion. Produced in video, radio and print, the ads were to run in eight Muslim nations during November 2002—the Holy Month of Ramadan—under formal sponsorship by the nonprofit Council of American Muslims for Understanding.

In addition to the $8.6 million in projected ad placements, embassies were to plan related activities in those countries and coordinate the launch of the "good will" campaign. The Muslims featured in the ads or other prominent Muslim-Americans would be available to travel to the target countries for speaking tours. Background materials on Muslims in the U.S. were produced in print and Web formats. Washington promised multi-media assistance to embassies based on their judgment on how to magnify the ad campaign locally. Each embassy identified target audiences, such as mothers, religious leaders, media reporters and students, that would maximize a change in perception.

Launching the Campaign

Neither State nor the U.S. Information Agency had extensive experience with ad campaigns, although USIA had conducted campaigns of persuasion. State's previous ad campaigns had aimed at specific results: soliciting information on suspected terrorists or recruiting Foreign Service officers. Shared Values' objective was much more ambitious: to change deep-seated feelings at a politically charged moment.

So State turned to the private sector. McCann-Erickson Worldwide produced the ads, testing both messages and featured spokespersons through its public relations affiliate, Weber-Shandwick Worldwide. Weber's branch offices organized focus groups in Jakarta and Cairo and vetted them with embassy staff in the target countries.

Beers failed, however, to anticipate the risk that her communication campaign might itself contribute to Muslim-American tension. When she revealed her plans for Shared Values to the press, that is exactly what happened. The campaign itself became an issue.

In the context of gathering war clouds over Iraq, a stalled Middle East peace process and arrests of Muslims in the U.S. and abroad, Arab governments and media organizations pushed back. In Lebanon, Morocco, Egypt, and Jordan, state-controlled national media refused to accept the ads. Moreover, several embassies curtailed their on-the-ground activities in the face of pressure from local governments or hostile local press reaction to "American propaganda." Beers pressed on, spending $4.8 million on media —half the projected amount—in Pakistan, Malaysia, Indonesia and Kuwait and on two pan-Arab satellite TV channels (not including Al-Jazeera). By January 2003, the ads stopped. Two months later, Beers resigned her post for health reasons.

State conducted no formal evaluation of the campaign. But the official embassy reporting available to this writer shows generally scant results. The "Issue Focus" report from INR's Media Reaction staff summarized world press reaction this way: "Many criticized the United States' perceived belief that it has the 'right to interfere to reform misconceptions in Arab societies' or to 'light a fire under the Islamic world [so it will] behave."

But in the one country where the campaign was carried out as planned, it succeeded. In Indonesia, the campaign did not become an issue and the embassy implemented it as intended. The full ad schedule ran with simultaneous local activities, including a Muslim-American speaker and a televised town hall meeting for young Indonesians and Americans. A professional post-campaign survey demonstrated that Indonesians recalled the Shared Values stories and understood their main message. In fact, the local survey company reported that our ads fared better than others advertising commercial products in Indonesia. More importantly, the embassy evaluated the initiative as a public diplomacy success and asset.

Beers clearly made a fatal mistake in the timing of the Shared Values campaign, and in how she presented it to the world press. In the Middle East her core message contrasted with real-world outcomes of U.S. policy. But in the Indonesian arena she proved that a persuasion campaign could work.

Rich Lessons to Be Learned

When the U.S. Information Agency was abolished in 1999, its divisions were transferred into different bureaus throughout the State Department, sacrificing centralized command and control. USIA's strategic communication office, which had coordinated campaigns of persuasion, was disbanded. Public diplomacy became essentially a bilateral enterprise, with weak levers of coordination from Washington. Finally, by bringing its public relations in-house, State lost the independent counsel that USIA had offered.

State's bilateral approach to foreign policy works against strategic communication, which often conflicts with embassy programs. Ambassador Edward P. Djerejian's report, "Public Diplomacy for the Arab and Muslim World," issued to the House of Representatives on Oct. 1, 2003, judged the Shared Values campaign to have been "well-conceived and based on solid research." The report laid part of the blame for its rejection in the Middle East at the feet of the embassies, which allegedly disapproved of the advertising techniques being used and failed to promote them vigorously.

Incoming public diplomacy executives can draw rich lessons from Shared Values:

- First, research-driven persuasive communication is a valuable component of public diplomacy. Television and paid advertising are powerful channels of communication that should be available when they are needed.
- Second, coordinated action by different embassies is indispensable when publics reach across national boundaries, as they usually do.
- Third, our PD officers need both the tools and the culture of measuring audiences and results. Formal evaluation is the final necessary step to any professional campaign.

To take public diplomacy to the next level, State must find a way to acquire professional expertise and advice from the private sector. A new under secretary can mitigate the problems and strengthen State's public diplomacy, but only by learning both from failures and successes of the past.

FSO Joe Johnson was Principal Deputy Coordinator of the International Information Programs Bureau from 2000 to 2003. The Bureau provides multi-channel communications services to embassies around the world. He presently serves as senior adviser in the eDiplomacy Office at the State Department.

Selected Bibliography

ABC News, *Good Morning America*, 14 December 2001.

Adams, Noah. "Profile: U.S. State Department defends an advertisement it placed in newspapers as part of the campaign against terrorism." *All Things Considered, National Public Radio*, 4 January 2002.

Anholt, Simon and Jeremy Hildreth. *Brand America: The Mother of All Brands*. London: Cyan Books, 2004.

"Arab youths wooed with U.S. magazine," *BBC News* 18 July 2003.

Arens, William F. *Contemporary Advertising*, 6th ed. Chicago:Irwin, 1996.

Babbie, E.R. *The Practice of Social Research*, 6th ed. Belmont, CA: Wadsworth, 1992.

Baran Stanley J. and Dennis K. Davis, *Mass Communication Theory:Foundations, Ferment and Future*, 3rd ed. Belmont, CA: Wadsworth, 2003.

Becker, Elizabeth. "In the war on terrorism, a battle to shape opinion." *The New York Times*, 11 November 2001, p. A1.

"Beers Bombs in the Middle East." *Marketing Week*, 1 March 2003, p. 3.

Beers, Charlotte. "Remarks to the National Press Club." Washington DC, 18 December 2002.

Beers, Charlotte. Testimony to the House Subcommittee on National Security, Emerging Threats and International Relations. 23 August 2004.

Bogart, Leo. *Cool Words, Cold War: A New Look at USIA's Premises for Propaganda*, Revised ed. Washington D.C.: American University Press, 1995.

Brown, Aaron. "Charlotte Beers." CNN's *NewsNight* 16 January 2003.

Brown, John. "Don't brand the U.S. Uncle Sam: The Backlash against Charlotte Beers' American Branding," posted on *CommonDreams.org*, 13 December 2004.

"Bush's Muslim propaganda chief quits." *CNN.com*, 4 March 2003.

Bush, George Walker. *Address before a joint session of the Congress on the United States response to the terrorist attacks of September 11*, September 2001. Washington, D.C.: Weekly Compilation of Presidential Documents.

Campbell, D.T. and J.C. Stanley. *Experimental and Quasi-experimental Designs and Research.* Skokie, IL: Rand McNally, 1963.

Capra, Frank. *The Name Above the Title: An Autobiography.* New York: Macmillan, 1971.

Carlson, Margaret. "Can Charlotte Beers sell Uncle Sam? Margaret Carlson on a former ad whiz's new gig." *Time On-line edition*, 14 November 2001.

Carlson, Peter. "America's Glossy Envoy." *The Washington Post*, 09 August 2003, sec. *Style*, p. A01.

Charney, Craig and Nicole Yakatan, "A new beginning: Strategies for a more fruitful dialogue with the Muslim world." Council on Foreign Relations, Inc.: New York, 2005.

Center for Media and Democracy, "Charlotte Beers," *Source Watch* Retrieved from http://www.sourcewatch.org/index.php?title= Charlotte_Beers

Crain, Rance. "Selling the idea of freedom the most important assignment for Beers." *Advertising Age,* 5 November 2001, p. 12.

Creel, George. *How We Advertised America: The First Telling of the Amazing Story of the Committee on Public Information that Carried the Gospel of Americanism to Every Corner of the Globe.* New York:Harper & Brothers, 1920.

"Diplomat Beers," *Advertising Age*, 1 October 2001, p. 16.

Djerejian, Edward P., Chariman, Report of the Advisory Group on Public Diplomacy in the Arab and Muslim World, *Changing Minds, Winning Peace: A New Strategic Direction for U.S. Public Diplomacy in the Arab and Muslim World,* 1 October 2003.

Fenton, Tom. *Bad News: The Decline of Reporting, the Business of News and the Danger to Us All. N*ew York:Harper Collins, 2005.

"From Uncle Ben's to Uncle Sam." *Economist*, Vol. 362, 23 February 2002, p. 70.

Garfield Bob. "Selling America." NPR radio interview with Charlotte Beers, 26 March 2004.

General Accounting Office. "State Department and the Broadcasting Board of Governors Expand Efforts in the Middle East but Face Significant Challenges." *GAO Highlights GAO-04-435T, a testimony before the Subcommittee on National Security, Emerging Threats, and International Relations.* 10 February 2004.

Gilgoff, Dan and Jay Tolson. "Losing friends? The departure of a top U.S. diplomat renews questions about how to fight anti-Americanism." *U.S. News & World Report*, 17 March 2003, p. 40.

Grimm, Matthew. "Now the loser: Brand USA." *Brandweek, 44,* 20 October 2003, p. 19.

Green, Fitzhugh. *American Propaganda Abroad.* New York: Hippocrene Books, 1988.

Hamilton, Matthew D., *Globalization and Anti-Americanism: A study of Singaporean college students.* Doctoral dissertation, Oklahoma State University, 2005.

Harris, Shane. "Brand U.S.A.," *Government Executive* (September 2003), p. 64.

Haskins, Jack B. "A precise notational system for planning and analysis." *Evaluation Review,* 5(1), 1981, pp. 33-50.

Haskins, Jack B. *How to Evaluate Mass Communication.* New York: Advertising Research Foundation, 1968.

Haskins, Jack B. and Alice Kendrick. *Successful Advertising Research Methods.* Chicago: NTC Books, 1993.

Helms, Ed. "What's it gonna take?" *The Daily Show with John Stewart on Comedy Central,* 13 April 2005.

Hillman, G. Robert. "White House public-relations office aims to tilt global spin." *The Dallas Morning News*, 19 March 2003, p. 19A.

House Budget Committee, "U.S. Representative Jim Nussle (R-IA) holds hearing on State Department fiscal year 2002 Budget Priorities," 15 March 2001.

Johnson, Joe B. "Public Diplomacy: What have we learned?" *Foreign Service Journal,* (April 2005), 13-14.

Jowett, Garth and Victoria O'Donnell. *Propaganda and Persuasion,* 3rd ed. Thousand Oaks, CA: Sage Publications, 1999.

Jowett, Garth. "Toward a Propaganda Analysis of the Gulf War." In *Desert Storm and the Mass Media*, edited by Bradley Greenberg and Walter Gantz. New Jersey: Hampton Press, 1993.

Katz, Elihu. "The two-step flow of communication: An up-to-date report of an hypothesis." *Public Opinion Quarterly* 21, (1957), 61-78.

Kendrick, Alice and Jami Fullerton. "Advertising as Public Diplomacy: Attitude change among international audiences." *Journal of Advertising Research* 44 (2004), 297-311.

Kendrick, Alice, Jami Fullerton, and Matthew D. Hamilton. "Reactions of Singaporeans to U.S. Public Diplomacy Advertising." Paper presented at the American Academy of Advertising Asia-Pacific Conference, Hong Kong, China. (2005, May).

Kendrick Alice and Jami Fullerton. "International Reaction to the Shared Values Initiative: The first U.S. advertising campaign to the Muslim world." (2004, March) Paper presented at the American Academy of Advertising 2004 Annual Conference, Baton Rouge, LA.

Kendrick Alice and Jami Fullerton. "A Propaganda Analysis of the Shared Values Initiative: The First US Advertising Campaign to the Muslim World." (2003, August). Paper presented at the Association for Education in Journalism and Mass Communication national convention, Kansas City, MO.

Kirkpatrick, Jerry. *In Defense of Advertising: Arguments from Reason, Ethical Egoism and Laissez Faire Capitalism.* Westport CT: Quorum Books, 1994.

Knoll, Jennifer. "U.S. hopes 'Hi' monthly will sway young Arab hearts and minds." *Jerusalem Report*, 8 September 2003, p. 7.

Kornblut, Anne E. "Problems of Image, Diplomacy Beset United States, *Boston Globe* 9 March 2003, p. A25.

Krugler, David F. *The Voice of America and the Domestic Propaganda Battles, 1945-1953.* Columbia, MO: University of Missouri Press, 2000.

Lambro, Donald. "Beaming up for Iraq's future." *The Washington Times,* 20 March 2003, p. A18.

Lasswell, Harold D. *Propaganda Technique in the World War.* New York: Peter Smith, 1927.

Lasswell, Harold D. "Propaganda." In *Encyclopedia of the Social Sciences*, Vol. 12, E. R. A. Seligman and A. Johnson, editors. New York: McMillian, 1937, 521-528.

Lau, Leslie. "U.S. Muslim ad drive on Malaysian TV 'a waste of time.'" *Straits Times Singapore*, 6 November 2002.

Lavidge, Robert J. and Gary A. Steiner, "A Model for Predictive Measurement of Advertising Effectiveness." *Journal of Marketing*, Vol.25 (October, 1961).

Lazarsfeld, Paul F., Bernard Berelson and Hazel Gaudet. *The People's Choice*. New York: Columbia University Press, 1948.

Lee, Alfred and Elizabeth Briant Lee. *The Fine Art of Propaganda*. New York: Harcourt, Brace and Company, 1939.

Lee, Matthew. "US aims to win over Arab youth with glossy new magazine," *Agence France Presse*, 12 August 2003.

Leser, Eric. "The United States does not succeed in improving their image." *Le Monde*, 17 March 2003.

Lieberman, Evelyn. "Closing the public information gap." *Washington Times*, 5 October 1999.

Lowery, Shearon and Melvin DeFleur, *Milestones in Mass Communication Research: Media Effects*, 3rd ed. (White Plains, NY: Longman, 1995).

McNeel, John M. "America, spare Arabs the spin," 9 June 2005, *International Herald Tribune*, p. 8.

Melillo, Wendy. "Defending Beers." *Adweek*, 10 March 2003, p. 24.

Melillo, Wendy. "The Peace Brokers: Ad execs can still help American diplomacy in the Arab world." *Adweek*, 23 June 2003, p 21.

Mitchell, Andrea "Bush hires advertising executive to pour out PR messages over Afghanistan." NBC Nightly News, 7 November 2001.

Neal, Terry M. "Image problem remains after departure." *Washingtonpost.com*, 6 March 2003,

Nelson, Richard. *A Chronology and Glossary of Propaganda in the United States*. Westport, CT and London: Greenwood Press, 1996.

Nemecek, Maureen J. "Speaking of America: The Voice of America, Its Mission and Message, 1942-1982." Doctoral Dissertation, University of Maryland, 1984.

O'Connell, Vanessa. "U.S. Suspends TV Ad Campaign Aimed at Winning Over Muslims." *Wall Street Journal*, 16 January 2003, p. A.1.

O'Keefe, Mark. "U.S. gives money to Muslim group to help image." *Christian Century*, 5 June 2002, p. 17.

Olson, James M. and Mark P. Zanna, "Attitudes and attitude change," *Annual Review of Psychology*, 44, 1993, p. 135.

Pew Research Center for the People and the Press. *What the World Thinks in 2002: How Global Publics View Their Lives, Their Countries, the World, America.* Washington, DC: The Pew Research Center, December 2002.

Pew Research Center for the People and the Press. *A Year After Iraq War: Mistrust of America in Europe Ever Higher, Muslim Anger Persists.* Washington, DC: The Pew Research Center, March 2004.

Powers, William. "Brand of the Free." *National Journal*, 33, 17 November 2001, p. 3577

Pratkanis, Anthony and Elliot Aronson. *Age of Propaganda: The everyday Use and Abuse of Persuasion,* rev. ed. New York:Henry Holt and Company, 2001.
"Public Diplomacy," *Online NewsHour*, 21 January 2003.

Rampton, Sheldon and John Stauber. *Weapons of Mass Deception: The Uses of Propaganda in Bush's War on Iraq.* New York: Jeremy P. Tarcher/Penguin, 2003.

Reinhard, Keith. Testimony to the House Subcommittee on National Security, Emerging Threats and International Relations, 23 August 2004.

Rosenshine, Allen "Now a word from America" *Advetising Age,* 18 February 2002, p. 15.

Schramm, Wilbur and Donald F. Roberts, eds. *The Process and Effects of Mass Communication.* Urbana, IL: University of Illinois Press, 1977.

Schubert, Atika. "U.S. tests charm offensive in Indonesia." *CNN.com*, 31 October 2002.

Sellers, Patricia ."Women, sex and power." *Fortune*, 5 August 1996, p. 42.

Severin, Werner J. and James W. Tankard. *Communication Theories, Origins, Methods and Uses in Mass Media,* 5th ed. New York:Longman, 2001.

Shays, Christopher. "Shays Statement for Hearing on 9/11 Commission Recommendations on Public Diplomacy" 23 August 2004.

Slavin, Barbara. "Sex, politics, but no rock 'n' roll: Powell talks openly with world youth." *USA Today*, 15 February 2002, p. B10.

Snow, Nancy. *Propaganda, Inc.: Selling America's Culture to the World.* 2nd edition. New York: Seven Stories Press, 2002.

Starr, Alexandra. "Charlotte Beers toughest sell." *Business Week*, December 2001, p. 56.

Teinowitz, Ira. "Beers draws mixed review after one year." *Advertising Age*, 23 September 2002, p 3.

Teinowitz, Ira. "Beers: State Dept. program misjudged." *Advertising Age*, 10 March 2003, p. 3.

Teinowitz, Ira. "Charlotte Beers to resign from State Department." *AdAge.com*, 3 March 2003.

Teinowitz, Ira. "Gov't eyes ad attack." *Advertising Age*, 15 October 2001, pp. 1, 49.

U.S. Department of State, "Briefing on the Rewards for Justice Program," 13 December 2001.

U.S. Senate Committee.on Foreign Relations. Hearing. "International campaign against terrorism," 25 October 2001.

U.S. Department of State Daily Press Briefing, Richard Boucher, Spokesman, 30 October 2002.

U.S. Department of State Daily Press Briefing, Richard Boucher, Spokesman, 16 January 2003.

U.S. Department of State Daily Press Briefing, Richard Boucher, Spokesman 3 March 2003.

U.S. Department of State, Office of Research, "U.S. image in the Islamic world: Policy is the problem," Ben Goldberg (ed), 26 November 2002.

U.S. Senate Committee on Foreign Relations. Hearing. "American public diplomacy and Islam to the U.S." 27 February 2003.

Waller, J. Michael. "U.S. not getting message out." *Insight on the News*, Vol. 19. 1 April-14 April 2003), 26-28.

Weisman, Steven R. "Powell aide quits position promoting U.S." *The New York Times*, 4 March 2003, 12.

Wise, Michael Z. "U.S. writers do cultural battle around the globe." *The New York Times*, 7 December 2002, 9.

Wolper, Gregg. "Wilsonian Public Diplomacy: The Committee on Public Information in Spain." *Diplomatic History,* Vol. 17, (1993), p. 17.

Yuen, C. W. "Leninism, Asian culture and Singapore." *Asian Profile*. June 1999.

Zaharna, Rhonda S. "American public diplomacy and the Islamic and Arab World: A communication update & assessment." Testimony before the Senate Committee on Foreign Relations, 27 February 2003.

Ziring, Lawrence, Jack C. Plano, and Roy Olton. *International Relations: A Political Dictionary,* 5th ed. Denver, CO: ABC-CLIO, 1995.

Index

9/11 (see September 11, 2001)

A

ABC television, 83, 84, 98, 111, 241, 248
advertising research, 152, 169, 178, 194, 243, 244
advertising effectiveness, 15, 147, 152, 194, 245
advertising (defined), 101-102
Advertising Age, 24, 103, 104, 110, 112, 116, 233, 242, 247
Adweek, 116, 197, 245
Afghanistan, 11, 26, 90, 156, 245
Al Hurra, 97, 98, 125, 209
Al Hayat, 38, 98, 108
Algeria, 33
American values, 20, 79, 154, 229, 230
Anholt, Simon, 111
Atta, Mohammed, 85
attitude change, 47, 67, 142, 146, 163, 169, 172, 202, 244, 246
attitudes toward America/United States, 78, 89, 140, 155, 156, 167, 172, 192, 195, 201, 204
audience measurement, 149
Azerbaijan, 34

B

Bahrain, 35, 79, 150
Baylor University, 21
BDA, (see Business for Diplomatic Action)
Beers, Charlotte (biography of) 21-23, (other mentions) 7, 8, 11-15, 19-27, 29-32, 34-36, 38-40, 51, 56, 69, 75, 76, 78, 80-84, 87-90, 94-96, 99, 101-104, 106, 108-112, 115-117, 120-131, 139, 140, 154, 158, 159, 161, 167, 181, 195-200, 202, 203, 205, 208-210, 212, 229-233, 235-238, 241-243, 245, 247
Bernays, Edward, 54
black propaganda, 47, 49
Boston Globe, 60, 104, 230, 244
Boucher, Richard (State Department spokesman), 26, 34, 38, 113, 117, 247
Brand America, 8, 20, 111, 112, 205, 233, 241
Brandweek, 99, 233, 243
British Broadcasting Corporation (BBC), 58, 80, 97, 109, 241
Broadcasting Board of Governors (BBG), 58, 61, 96, 97, 120, 156, 243

Brown, Aarron, 4, 5, 126, 229
Bush, George W. (President), 23-26, 31, 33, 36, 71, 77, 88, 94, 101, 106, 111, 112, 182, 197, 230, 231, 235, 242, 245
Business for Diplomatic Action (BDA), 120, 126, 205, 213, 233

C

Cable News Network (CNN), 34, 36, 38, 98, 117, 137, 138, 242, 246
Cantril, Hadley (also see War of the Worlds), 62-64, 67
Carpenter, David, 83
Catholic Church, Roman, 45, 46
CBS television, 63, 64, 111, 147
Cheney, Dick (Vice President), 200
church and state, 29, 31, 207
Clinton, Bill (President), 78
Cold War, 19, 20, 43, 49, 52, 57-60, 89, 118, 119, 178, 241
Committee on Public Information (Creel committee), 51, 53, 55, 60, 242, 247
communication model, 26, 142
Congress, 4, 15, 24, 36, 39, 44, 56, 59-61, 97, 116, 118, 139, 154, 242
consumer research, 27, 159
Council of American Muslims for Understanding (CAMU), 30, 31, 33, 34, 36, 70, 91, 144, 204, 236
Creel, George (also see Committee on Public Information), 53, 55
Cyprus, 79

D

Daily Show with John Stewart, 112, 243
Dallas Morning News, The, 104, 243
Davis, Elmer, 55
demographic differences, 175

Djerejian Report, 29, 118, 119
Djerejian, Edward, 29

E

Egypt, 34, 35, 79, 92, 107, 124, 158, 171, 237
embassies/embassy, 35, 36, 51, 87, 88, 94, 107, 117, 118, 123, 125, 127, 140, 158, 159, 197, 198, 212, 236-240
experimental research/experiments, 5, 13, 15, 43, 66, 167, 168, 171, 178, 195, 202, 214

F

Fandy, Mamoun, 38, 108, 109, 132, 207, 215
favorability ratings, 155, 156
focus groups, 113, 114, 157-159, 162, 237
Fulbright programs, 51, 56, 61, 110, 201

G

Gaza Strip, 79
Greece, 79
gross rating points (GRPs), 148-150
Gulfstream Aerospace Corporation, 20

H

Hammuda, Abdul, 95, 96, 100
Hasan, Malik, 30
Harvard Business School, 21
hearts and minds, 79, 97, 140, 162, 167, 201-203, 213, 244
Hi Magazine, 78-80, 125, 130, 209

Hierarchy of Effects, 152, 153, 202
Hovland, Carl, 66, 67, 144, 146
Hughes, Karen, 80, 103

I

Indonesia, 27-29, 34-36, 38, 39, 91-94,
    107, 108, 122, 129, 137, 150, 151,
    156-159, 162, 163, 167, 168, 178,
    195, 206, 214, 238, 246
International Herald Tribune, 126, 245
Islam/Islamic, 19, 29-31, 34, 38, 39, 43,
    90, 94, 105-110, 111, 119, 128, 159,
    161, 168, 188, 190, 203, 236, 238,
    247, 248
Ismail, Rawai, 33
Israel, 11, 79, 98, 107, 108, 117, 193

J

Johnson, Joe B., 4, 5, 8, 127, 235
Jordan, 34, 35, 79, 91-93, 150, 156, 237

K

Kazakhstan, 11, 34
Kennedy, John F. (President), 59
Kenya, 35
Korean War, 56
Kuwait, 35, 36, 79, 91, 93, 107, 150,
    151, 206, 238

L

Lasswell, Harold D., 46, 62, 244
Le Monde, 40, 105, 109, 207, 245
Lebanon, 35, 79, 91-93, 95, 98, 107,
    150, 237
Lieberman, Evelyn, 23, 61

Lippmann, Walter, 62

M

Magic Bullet, 62
Malaysia, 35, 36, 91, 93, 105-107, 150,
    151, 206, 238
Matalin, Mary, 200
McCann-Erickson advertising agency,
    14, 32, 34, 39, 91-93, 113, 116,
    148-151, 150, 158-160, 162, 202,
    206, 237
media effects, 64, 67, 144, 245
media plan, 91, 148, 200, 205, 206
Morocco, 79, 91-93, 107, 150, 237
MTV (Music Television), 12, 76-78, 96
Murrow, Edward R., 8, 59
Muslim Life in America, 31, 75, 91, 94,
    107, 154, 163, 199
Muslim Americans, 68, 69, 110, 158
Muslims, 19, 29-31, 33, 34, 36, 39,
    69-71, 90-92, 94, 95, 104-109, 111,
    112, 122, 124, 127, 128, 138, 140,
    144, 158, 162, 168, 169, 171-184,
    186-193, 204, 230, 233, 236, 237,
    245

N

National Press Club, 99, 200, 241
National Public Radio (NPR), 86, 96,
    122, 210, 241, 242
National Institutes of Health, 19, 31, 33,
    236
Nazi Germany, 43, 49
NBC television, 26, 245
Nelson, Richard, 10, 50
network of terrorism, 87
New York Times, The, 25, 89, 101, 102,
    117, 124, 147, 201, 241, 247

New York Magazine, 20, 24
newspaper(s), 14, 31, 38, 40, 58, 64, 66,
    90-93, 98, 105, 106, 109, 142, 147,
    148, 207

O

Office of War Information, 55, 57
Oklahoma State University, 15, 168,
    243
Ogilvy & Mather, 21
Oman, 35, 79, 150
opinion polls, 155, 236
opinion leader, 147
Osama bin Laden, 81, 182

P

Pakistan, 35, 36, 91-93, 105, 107, 150,
    151, 156, 203, 206, 238
Pentagon, 36, 231
persuasion theory, 67, 142
persuasive communication, 13, 15, 46,
    50, 68, 71, 127, 142, 143, 147, 236,
    239
Pew Research Center for the People and
    the Press (results of surveys) 110,
    156, 246
Powell, Colin L. (Secretary of State), 5,
    8, 12, 17, 19, 20, 23, 24, 36, 39, 40,
    76-78, 81, 83, 87, 101, 103, 115,
    117, 130, 197, 200, 213-215, 229,
    230, 246, 247
press briefing, 26, 34, 38, 83, 113, 117,
    247
propaganda (see especially Chapter 2),
    5, 12, 14, 25, 30, 35, 38, 43-50,
    52-55, 57, 58, 60-63, 65, 67, 68, 71,
    98, 101, 110, 112, 117, 143, 146,
    179-182, 190, 191, 196, 199, 201,
    238, 241-246

propaganda devices, 67, 68
public diplomacy (see especially
    Chapter 2), 4, 5, 7, 8, 12-15, 19, 20,
    23-25, 27, 29, 35, 36, 38, 39, 43, 44,
    47, 50-53, 57, 58, 60, 61, 71, 72, 75,
    76, 87, 96-99, 101, 103, 107-111,
    114-121, 123, 125-129, 137, 139,
    140, 159, 161, 163, 167, 169,
    195-197, 199-202, 204-206, 208,
    209, 211-214, 229-231, 235,
    238-240, 242-244, 246-248
public relations, 4, 51, 54, 55, 76, 98,
    104, 106, 118, 180, 181, 211, 237,
    239
public opinion polls, 155
Public Broadcasting Service (PBS), 35,
    38, 108, 109

Q

Qatar, 35, 79, 98, 150

R

radio, 14, 44, 53, 55, 58, 59, 63-65, 75,
    83, 84, 86, 90, 92, 96, 97, 121, 122,
    125, 148, 209, 210, 236, 241, 242
Radio Sawa, 96, 97, 125, 209
Ramadan, 30, 36, 90, 115, 123, 208
religion, 28, 29, 31, 33, 106, 161, 171,
    180, 183, 184, 189, 190, 236
religious tolerance, 29, 30, 111, 122,
    154, 163
Rewards for Justice, 75, 80, 81, 83-85,
    210, 247
Rice, Condoleezza (National Security
    Adviser), 76, 230
Roper polls, 29, 110, 157, 236
Ross, Christopher (Ambassador), 8, 76,
    101, 128-130, 197

Rumsfeld, Donald (Secretary of
    Defense), 76
Russia, 170

S

Saudi Arabia, 27-29, 35, 79, 107, 150
Senate Foreign Relations Committee,
    17, 103, 109, 117, 215
September 11, 2001 (9/11), 11, 20, 24,
    40, 70-72, 75, 76, 85, 87, 89, 96, 98,
    119, 120, 128, 129, 155, 167, 179,
    180, 183, 184, 188, 189, 204, 207,
    212, 215, 229, 246
sleeper effect, 144, 146
Snow, Nancy, 52, 110, 197
source credibility, 31, 144, 204, 205
Southern Methodist University, 11, 29,
    89
Soviet Union (USSR), 19, 57, 58, 233
State Department (U.S. Department of
    State), 7, 8, 12-15, 20, 23, 24, 26,
    29-32, 34-36, 38, 44, 51, 55-57, 60,
    61, 69, 71, 75, 76, 78-81, 83, 85-89,
    92, 94-98, 101, 103, 104, 106, 108,
    110, 111, 113, 115-118, 120, 121,
    125, 127-131, 138, 139, 141,
    148-151, 154, 156, 160, 162, 163,
    193, 195, 197-200, 202-204,
    207-211, 232, 239-241, 243, 247
Sudan, 79
SVI spots, 13, 29, 35, 36, 39, 44, 69, 71,
    95, 107, 121, 123, 128, 129, 138,
    142, 144, 150, 151, 154, 156, 160,
    163, 173, 186, 195, 202
Syria, 8, 76, 79, 118, 128

T

Tanzania, 35
Tatham advertising agency, 21

terrorism, 1-5, 14, 15, 25, 71, 81, 82, 86,
    87, 103, 116, 119, 195, 214, 230,
    241, 247
terrorist attacks, 24, 96, 119, 242
Thompson, J. Walter, 21, 22
Tunisia, 79, 107

U

U.S. Department of State (see State
    Department)
Uncle Ben's Rice, 21, 24, 103, 116, 233
United States Information Agency
    (USIA), 19, 20, 51, 52, 57-61, 87,
    98, 110, 125, 139, 197, 211, 232,
    237, 239
United Arab Emirates, 35, 79, 107, 150
University of Michigan, 13, 169
University of Southwestern Louisiana,
    21

V

Voice of America (VOA), 44, 57-59, 61,
    96, 97, 244, 245

W

Wall Street Journal, The, 36, 109, 113,
    230, 245
war on terrorism, 4, 5, 14, 15, 25, 71,
    116, 195, 214, 241
War of the Worlds, 63, 65
Washington Times, The, 61, 97, 244,
    245
Washington Post, The, 25, 79, 83, 242
Weber Shandwick, 106, 107
Welles, Orson, 63
West Bank, 79

white propaganda, 47-50, 58
Wilson, Woodrow (President), 53
World War I, 43, 45, 46, 53, 55
World War II, 43, 55, 144
World Trade Center, 36, 89
Writers on America, 88, 89

Y-Z

Yemen, 79
Zerhouni, Elias (Director of the National
    Institutes of Health), 19, 31, 33, 236